Beautiful
IN HIS
Time

STORIES BY WOMEN WITH BEAUTIFUL
EXPERIENCES OF TRUSTING GOD.

COMPILED BY

SOLA MACAULAY

Beautiful in His time

Copyright © 2020 by Sola Macaulay

Unless otherwise noted, all Scripture is taken from the King James Version
of the Bible.

Paperback: ISBN 13: 978-978-986-560-4
ISBN 10: 978-986-560-0

Design by: Artcom Design Int'l +234-08028487272
Histiara Publishing +234-07080317274

REVIEWS

2020 has been a year like no other and getting to read **Beautiful in His Time** at such a time like this must have been divinely orchestrated due to the tremendous impact it has made in my life.

Beautiful in His Time renewed my hope, faith, strength and trust in my heavenly Father. The conversational style of the book made me feel I was having chitchat with my friends. I was so drawn to the stories that I couldn't drop the book till I got to the end.

The stories demonstrated God's love for us time and time again. They revealed the power of God at work in diverse circumstances and strengthened the fact that there's nothing impossible for God to do in our lives. If only we allow Him by simply trusting and surrendering all unto Him even when our situations look the bleakest. Just like any relationship, our relationship with our heavenly Father must be based on our total trust in Him.

Thank you, Sola Macaulay for this awesome read!

Titlayo Adeyemo
Pharmacist and Craft Coach
www.instagram.com/pinklemon.ng

This definitely must be on your reading list for 2020. It's full of stories that resonate with our experience as women. In a world that is tired and worn out with the pandemic it rekindles our trust in a loving God who makes all things beautiful in their time. It's Sola Macaulay at her best!

Debola Oni

"And they overcame the devil by the blood of the lamb and the words of their testimonies." Rev.12: 11

The testimonies of these beautiful women are diverse. Ranging from breaking forth into a new era of calling despite a bitter experience in marriage, achieving conception after three years of waiting. There are also the miracles of having children; which seemed medically impossible with prior reports of hyperthyroidism and uterine fibroid. There was a lady sustained by God in her academic pursuit. The desire to have a son and to win the numerous battles over the life of this son pushed another lady back to the God she initially rejected. The testimony of a young lady who met the God of love that makes everything Beautiful in Him Time despite the twists and turns of life.

"Thou hast caused men to ride over our heads; we went through fire and through water but thou brought us out into a wealthy place." Psalm 66:12

These women have gone through fire and water, but they've eventually gotten to their wealthy place. These stories will serve as evidence of God's goodness and faithfulness to millions of men and women who are willing to hold on to God's words, walking by faith and not by sight. Thank you wonderful women for sharing your stories of faith. Thank you Sola Macaulay for yielding to God's voice on compiling these chronicles of trust in the living God.

Dr. Adebimpe Ogunmodede

The Trust Chronicles was an interesting read of learning to trust in God's faithfulness even when the chips are down and you can't see what's coming next. As humans, it is only natural to want to know the full extent of what's coming. But if you know what is coming how have you expressed faith? Like Jesus said to Thomas, you believe because you see, but blessed are those who without seeing believe. This for me was a lesson in trust, faith and continued reliance on God even when things don't go our way like the lady whose mum died.

Mrs Ogunbanjo

INTRODUCTION

Dear Reader,

I commend **BEAUTIFUL IN HIS TIME**, book 3 of The Trust Chronicles to you. It is often said that walking with God is an adventure of faith – a journey that builds a robust knowledge of God and His character. Of the many names of God – trust is often synonymous with His character.

The timing of God is sometimes not palatable for us. We wish God to move now, in our own time and way. Some things work out just as we hoped, while most things don't work out as planned. Yet behind these seeming 'disappointments' is a grander plan. God who has the blueprint of our lives from the beginning of existence moves time and events to fall in sync with exactly how He has planned it and at the end of the day, everything works out beautiful, even the not-so-expected events in our lives.

God doesn't often give us a peek into the delays, the detours of ahead, but He requires our absolute trust in order to fulfill His purpose in our lives.

These stories will make you pause and help you see how in navigating our lives, God is always there, causing all things to work out for our good and making everything *beautiful in His time*.

We hope that you will be refreshed as you read, and your faith renewed in God. Remember that He is God, He loves you with an everlasting love and His plans are always to prosper us and give us a beautiful ending.

Blessings,
Sola Macaulay
2020

DEDICATION

Dedicated to the woman who has placed all her trust and time in God's hands.

"We must cease striving and trust God to provide what He thinks is best and in whatever time He chooses to make it available. But this kind of trusting doesn't come naturally. It's a spiritual crisis of the will in which we must choose to exercise faith."
— Swindoll Charles R.

Eccl: 3:11
Yet God has made everything beautiful for its own time. He has planted eternity in the human heart, but even so, people cannot see the whole scope of God's work from beginning to end. (NLT)

Romans 8:28
And we know that in all things God works for the good of those who love him, who[a] have been called according to his purpose. (NIV)

CONTENT

1

HE MAKES ALL THINGS BEAUTIFUL IN HIS TIME

TOBI EYINADE

I have always grappled with the concept of time. I don't like waiting; the process of being in limbo, with uncertainty staring me in the eyes, can be gruelling. However, God has taught me major lessons with the one thing I dislike the most.

I've always been considered an early starter. Even though I was the most unserious in every standard in comparison to my siblings, my journey has mostly been marked with quick acceleration. I gained admission into university without a breather. In the same year I ended high school, I was in my dream university. Though I was not studying my dream course, I eventually came to terms with being a wounded lawyer during my second year and promised to make the most of the entire experience.

Perhaps, on the basis of events happening in quick succession for me early in life, I just assumed I was going to settle down at a young age. See my "almighty formula":

Age 20: Be done with my four-year degree program
Age 21: Wrap up NYSC
Age 22: Have my dream job and be married.

Alas, the ways of God are never the ways of men (Isaiah 55:9). In a bid to live my fantasy, I started dating at barely seventeen. And it wasn't a mindless relationship; it had marriage in view (or so I thought). He was, as a matter of fact, the first man I ever loved. A medical doctor, his career path looked straightforward. He didn't have to compete so hard in the labour market to get a job.

And so the journey to courting began. The first two years were not so bad based on my low standards. Then came the third year when it became glaring I was in a dysfunctional relationship. The man I was supposedly meant to spend the rest of my life with had repeatedly cheated on me. I'd always console myself with the thought that it meant something that he always came back to me to admit his wrongs.

"I don't know how it all happened. She visited me. I was vulnerable because you don't allow us to do these things. If you do, I won't have gone seeking or be doing such with other women." Those were the tones his explanation typically took. They were also my cues and red flags to walk away. But I was deeply scared and scarred to leave. Also, the picture-perfect image of having a beautiful home of mine at age 22 risked being distorted. I didn't want that.

And so I stayed in an emotionally abusive relationship for four years and held on tight to the hopes that things would change or get better with time. Forgetting that it is an effort in futility salvaging what was not meant to be in the first place.

2

The tell-tale signs of a bad relationship will always ooze. No matter how hard one tries to conceal them. It didn't take so much effort for people around me to realise I was unhappy and my relationship was a ticking time bomb.

Just in time, God Himself orchestrated my liberation and made the scales fall off my eyes. The supposed "Mr Right" confessed with gory details the tales of his escapades with other countless ladies. He had even, at this point, begun to blaspheme and tilt towards atheism – openly professing his belief in science and not the almighty God. It dawned on me that he was long sinking into a well and any attempt to save him would find me in the same well.

I realised I was casting my pearls before a swine. Matt 7:6 was the word that empowered me to walk away. I reckoned that beyond just achieving the self-imposed ambition of marrying at 22, it just was not worth sacrificing my self-worth and sentencing myself to a lifetime of misery in exchange. I needed to find myself and discover purpose.

My journey to healing was a three-year roller coaster ride. There were moments of utter despair, anger at myself for ignoring the red flags and not walking away early. Several months of total disdain at the male species passed. I began to hate *love* and just couldn't wrap my head around it. I remember I'd see a public display of healthy, genuine affection from a couple and couldn't understand why anyone would look at another human with so much joy and satisfaction. Simply insert all the many signs of a heart-wretched person here. That was me for three years after I walked out of the relationship with my supposed "Mr Right".

Matthew 7:6 "Do not give dogs what is sacred; do not throw your pearls to pigs. If you do, they may   trample them under their feet, and turn and tear you to pieces. [New International Version

THEN I MET THE GOD OF LOVE

What is wonderful about God's love is that it is constant. It's ever there to embrace us warmly without condemnation whenever we choose to accept it.

For a long time, I failed to acknowledge the pain I felt and had a hard time revisiting the events of the past. I never deemed it fit to talk about my deep-seated insecurity and lack of trust. Apparently, this also reflected in my walk with God. I'd pray but won't believe that leaving my worries and plans at the foot of the Father was enough. I'd obsess over the issues in anxiety just because I didn't want to deal with the eventual disappointment of things not working out the way I wanted. Oh, I was a control freak! I played "God" over my life and never rested in the thought that unlike men, He is different and can be trusted.

Gradually, I began to tire as my strength and calculations in many circumstances began to fail me. I solemnly realised I couldn't see beyond my nose and it's better to trust God who sees the end right from the beginning. He began to show Himself strongly in my affairs. God was so mindful of me; I could see His love vividly beyond reasonable doubt.

> *"For when God made the promise to Abraham, He swore [an oath] by Himself, since He had no one greater by whom to swear, saying, "I WILL SURELY BLESS YOU AND I WILL SURELY MULTIPLY YOU." And so, having patiently waited, he realized the promise [in the miraculous birth of Isaac, as a pledge of what was to come from God]. Indeed men swear [an oath] by one greater than themselves, and with them [in all*

disputes] the oath serves as confirmation [of what has been said] and is an end of the dispute. In the same way God, in His desire to show to the heirs of the promise the unchangeable nature of His purpose, intervened and guaranteed it with an oath, so that by two unchangeable things [His promise and His oath] in which it is impossible for God to lie, we who have fled [to Him] for refuge would have strong encouragement and indwelling strength to hold tightly to the hope set before us." (Hebrews 6:13-18 AMP)

I STOPPED PUTTING GOD IN A BOX

In 2018, my sister, who has always held me up in the place of prayer, reached out to me concerning a program she wanted me to attend. I was livid because I felt it was too early to start going from one Prayer Mountain to another concerning an issue that wasn't within my control. *"My matter never reach that* level *na,"* I retorted.

I guess my nonchalance bothered her. She had always feared I had given up concerning that aspect of my life. Truth be told, I had come to a place of indifference about marriage. I just wanted to love up on myself, be the best in my career and business. I didn't give a hoot about men because of the awful ones I had met – they were downright not what God wanted for me or cases of me not opening up my heart to receive their love.

Nonetheless, out of sheer curiosity, I attended this program called SUPERNATURAL MARRIAGE COURSE. Trust me, even the name of the program put me off. I mean, why do I have to invoke God to do something by attending a program first? Nevertheless, I attended to *fulfil all righteousness* and make my sister happy.

SMC turned out to be a far cry from what I thought – one of those relationship seminars where they analyse and tell you everything that is wrong with you and stopping you from getting "Mr Right". SMC was a faith seminar instead – a place of reigniting an intimate walk with the Father. It was an altar of fellowship and communion with the Holy Spirit. Rather than nonchalance, I surrendered and embraced His perfect will for me.

It was during this period all the strange checklists; weird stereotypes and belief systems that were not rooted in God's word started changing. (Hebrews 4:12) I held on to my confessions and fully embraced my waiting phase with a paradigm shift. This time, I understood that waiting is not a state of being in limbo or inactivity. It is perfectly accepting God's timing and trusting Him daily to bring His word to pass. I unlearned and relearned so many things through the help of the Holy Spirit.

I was so caught up with doing good, enjoying God and thriving in different aspects of my life that when the man God wanted for me showed up in the last quarter of 2019, I was basking in God and was able to decipher and receive him as His gift of love to me.

He turned out to be everything I ever prayed for and more. It's like God was eavesdropping on the salient thoughts in my heart and melded them and so much more into one person. (Romans 8:26)

Those innermost *groanings* that are hard to utter in the place of

---

Hebrews 4:12 For the word of God is alive and active. Sharper than any double-edged sword, it penetrates even to dividing soul and spirit, joints and marrow; it judges the thoughts and attitudes of the heart. [New International Version]

Romans 8:26 In the same way, the Spirit helps us in our weakness. We do not know what we ought to pray for, but the Spirit himself intercedes for us through wordless groans. [New International Version]

prayer, nights with tear-soaked pillows, moments of anguish when people made unsolicited remarks on how I was too good to be single, men that felt my ambition and expectations were a bit too much; all came together to bring me into God's perfect will for my life.

These days, I look back and I'm thankful to Abba for my journey. The twists, turns, waiting and pain on the way sure didn't sit down well with me at that moment, but it moulded me into a better version of myself – a woman who fiercely believes that God makes EVERYTHING beautiful in HIS time.

ABOUT THE AUTHOR

Tobi Eyinade is the co-founder of Rovingheights bookstore. She holds a bachelor's degree in English from Obafemi Awolowo University and is a conduit that seeks to transform minds by rekindling their interest in books. She is currently pursuing an MBA program at the University of Surrey, Guildford and thoroughly enjoys deep moments of worship and praise to Abba.

HE RESTORES MY SOUL

ELE MOMOH

This is a story of soul healing.

This story may seem disjointed but I pray you get the picture in the end. It's one of those experiences that are not easily told in five or six pages, or even five or six months. It's my story of realising I was living below God's best for me and going through a difficult but rewarding journey of soul healing. This helped me come into the understanding and experience of God's love, peace, and goodness.

This may seem like a simple story (which may not have many details) of recognising I was at the receiving end of different kinds of abuse, and trying to get out. But the story is more than that. It's me talking about how I was led to find out who I really am and part of why I'm here because I got uncomfortable.

You see, I've observed many abuse trends in recent times. Abuse in church, in the workplace, at home, and on the streets. No matter the form it takes, abuse violates the soul. But I've also observed, especially when it comes to church, that many people lean toward their version of righteous indignation and forget that trying to bring down an abuser does not heal the abused. And abuse is a two-way street. Sometimes, we let ourselves be abused either out of ignorance or neglect. I was lied to, gas-lighted, harmed verbally and socially, coerced sexually, disrespected and had some of the things I liked about myself used against me by someone I'd grown to love, honour and respect. I haven't told this story to many people but most who hear it tend to react righteously on my behalf. But when I spoke to Mrs Sola Macaulay about it, she said words I'll never forget. She said, "God will handle him, but I'm concerned about you."

She explained what she meant but it was so much more than that to me. It was as though God was ripping a veil off my eyes and reminding me that regardless of all that had happened, He was concerned about me. Not just because I'd been abused, but also because I was unwilling to admit it. Sure, I was making myself tell it, but in my heart, I hadn't accepted it. And I was unwilling to admit it because I was ashamed. And I was ashamed because I thought I deserved to have been treated that way. And I thought I deserved bad treatment because I wasn't fully aware of my worth.

What I share in the rest of this story is a collage of my prayers and desires and thoughts I penned down over a period of time. They all began to make sense to me when this healing journey started. It was more than just healing from abuse, I repeat; it was a route to discovery. It was God's light shining on me and in me, to see beyond a bad incident into, for lack of a better word, more.

21ˢᵗ June 2019
These are interesting times...

It's a season of refining and recognition. It's a season of harvest and hard work. It's a defining season — the soul is being put to the test.

Perspective is paramount.
Harvest is in sight. In fact, I'm standing amidst ripe fruit, right there in the fields. And temptations are many. I'm tempted to give up. I am tempted to give in. I am tempted to lash out. I am tempted to withdraw. I am tempted to be mean and unforgiving. I am tempted to remember the painful past. I am tempted to laze around.

Some days, it's not a temptation — I am well and truly overwhelmed.

I don't want to keep some of my secrets alone anymore. I want to share my life, my heart. I want to belong in a meaningful and worthwhile way with someone... I want to write my heart out and then some without having to be tamed. I want that fire... And I will have it all.

26th June 2019
What do I do, Father? How do I handle this? Help me. You know, long ago, You've known me and You made me. I'm not cut out for this. Help me. I don't want to fight a servant of Yours, especially this one, ever again. I'd rather leave him to You. He's Your son and Your servant. You know how best to reach him and save him. I'm ready to move out of the way, oh God. And I want to walk Your path for me without tension and apprehension. I want to learn Your way for me. I want to come to know that there are men I can trust that way in this world. I want to know that the way I am is not a mistake – that my body and my heart can be given as one and that there is someone to whom that means something...

27ᵗʰ June 2019

Psalm 62
I stand silently to listen for the One I love, waiting as long as it takes for the Lord to rescue me.
For God alone has become my Saviour.
He alone is my safe place; His wrap-around presence always protects me.
For He is my champion defender, there's no risk of failure with God. So why would I let worry paralyse me, even when troubles multiply around me? Trust only in God every moment!

Tell Him all your troubles and pour out your heart-longings to Him. Believe me when I tell you – He will help you!

There are secret things my heart desires, and I must calm down, be still, and hope only in God. He alone is my help forever.

16ᵗʰ September 2019

Dear God,
I don't want to be a crutch anymore. I don't want to be a crutch anymore. I want peace. I want purity. I want my choices to be mine. I want the freedom to fill my mind with other stuff, to believe that there is goodness in me, to believe that I'm truly worth it. I want the freedom to want what I want without shame. I want the heart position it takes to tell THIS story in the most God-inspired and honest way possible. I want to know that I'm worth more than closed doors, darkened rooms, muted sounds, hired halls, and playacting. I want to be a whole person.
P.S: Real victory comes when you, Ele, change your mind.

21ˢᵗ September 2019

Dear God,
I need You. Desperately.
Every attempt without You is an attempt. We never get far.

I'm bringing my cares, concerns and burdens. The overwhelming thoughts and feelings I can't fight on my own. "Faith is living trust in the living God." There is no one else I can trust not to hurt, disappoint or misunderstand and judge. You're the only one – right now – with whom I am safe. So I run to You... Help me, Lord. My soul is in need of softening, of tenderness, of openness... Help me to forgive, to let go of these pains, these hurts and misconceptions. Lead me to see You instead of the criticism/applause of men. Give me understanding into spiritual things so that I'm not confused by doctrine or example. Give me Your light so I'm not condemned when I hear talk about "If you were sowing your seeds" or "The good girl syndrome" or any of those things that make my heart fail within me.

30th September 2019

Dear God,
...So you see how much I've entertained this thing unwittingly. But I don't want to anymore. There's a whole grand life I have to love – a hundred thousand things to see! I want to focus. I want to pay attention to God and to this life that I've been gifted to live. I want to leave pettiness and immaturity and laziness and time-wasting behind. I want to step up and stand tall... I don't want to be the person playing in the same yard for 20 years with no change or improvement. I want to be the person who takes things seriously, takes people seriously and gives and does all in my power to make this life worthwhile. I want to be the person who loves wholeheartedly and is unafraid of the shadows that others bring with them. I don't

want to be the person saying one thing and living another. I want to see what I'm truly made of. I want to see how large my heart is... I want more out of life. I want more love, more grace, more faith, more patience, more wisdom, more kindness, more steadfastness, more of all that this great God has for me.

You see why I can't trade my heart? So I fight for my heart.

10ᵗʰ October 2019
Psalm 69:33
Let all who seek God's help be encouraged. For the Lord hears the cries of the needy; He does not despise His imprisoned people.

I had an argument with this person who I was both praying for and praying to get away from, and decided, seemingly out of the blue, that I wasn't going back. I hadn't prayed about it in a while; I didn't even plan to do it, but it felt like a veil came off my eyes and suddenly, I knew it was the right thing to do and I knew it was time.

But there, the difficult journey began. The one where I had to open myself up and let the darkness out so the light could come in. With the help of a precious woman of God, I got into therapy and my therapy helped me figure out what I wanted out of the experience. This was it: I look forward to answers, healing, freedom, purpose and the restoration of my dreams.

And week after week, as she guided me toward the light, I began to open up. I started seeing places in me that had been beaten and broken and courageously opened them to God's love. Even harder was the correction of the Holy Ghost because you wouldn't imagine an abused person needing correction, right? But I needed it. I needed to see that in some areas, the person doing the lying and manipulating was doing his thing but in other areas, I had come to think of myself too low — even in my own eyes. I thought I knew God loved me, and to a degree, I did. But I needed to be corrected about my worth. I needed to be shown that God does not value someone else more than me. I needed to be shown that God is concerned about me — that I matter to Him. I needed to understand that my wholeness was important to Him. I needed to understand that in this relationship of ours, God wasn't looking down on me. He wasn't hiding somewhere, snickering at me, telling me in bad jokes that I am not made for anything special. And in slow goings, learning to be honest, learning to say out loud that I was wrong and learning to acknowledge that I was hurt and that I needed healing. Learning to be okay with seeing myself through God's eyes — worthy.

31st March 2020
Lemme find small honesty inside my heart today.

I do not dislike this period at all... I 'wish' I'd wake up tomorrow inside next week with COVID gone, my sanity and wholeness intact, a job to go to and all the other things I prayed for. But that's not going to happen and I'm cool with that.

My feelings will become my friends because by the help of God, I will know and understand them for what they are at various points of my existence here. God is good. I am closer to answers, healing, freedom, restoration and purpose than I was a year ago. He is truly the Portion of my inheritance and the Maintainer of my destiny.

I will own this and I am owning this thing. I will become a smooth, sweet blend of steel, wisdom, and gentleness, and all my hurt and pain and loneliness will ground into plaster. I will paint the dry walls and they will be laid with precious stones and dignified ornaments. I will be confident again. I will trust again. I will love again. I will have meaning again. I will be joyful and contagiously impactful again. I will have purpose and I will live the best life God planned for me on this earth.

The Lord is my God.
He is my Fortress; I will never be shaken.
He is my Strength.
He is my Father.
He is the Portion of my inheritance and the Maintainer of my destiny.
He is Captain of my life, my soul, and my destiny.
I belong to this Mighty God.

My rants and prayers in this season remind me of David's. I've never encountered a character so unashamed of bearing it all and embracing God with His entire being. I admire the honesty with which he spoke to God in the scriptures, letting Him into his issues and praising Him for deliverance at the same time.

If it isn't evident, I used the Psalms a lot. Many days and nights, when I had no prayers to pray, I would read the Psalms – chapters sixteen, eighteen, twenty-three, thirty-four, and sixty-two. The Psalms got me through times of anger, guilt, shame and other things I can't remember. Abuse, which I know I haven't much talked about, means to put to wrong or improper use. It also means to use or treat so as to injure or damage. It means to attack in words. And it means to deceive.

Many of us have experienced some form of abuse or the other. Maybe you've been gas-lighted. Or your boundaries have been violated. Or you've been made fun of but told, "Ah, we're just playing." But the words cut you deeply. Much more than my empathy, I can assure you that we have a Father who sees, who knows and who understands. He does not love some more than others. He is never okay with people hurting people. He will always heal the broken-hearted and bind up their wounds (Isaiah 61:3-4). He will always heal the things wrong with us (Isaiah 53:4-5, MSG).

I am still on this healing journey; I have begun to see answers to prayers I made. Unexpectedly, the things I wrote in *The Hand You Hold* started to surface. And I realised that this journey is long. God does show His love and mercy in amazing ways through people, but you have to be willing to let the past go and embrace what He offers. And that's what this story is about: a healing journey in my soul because "I sought the Lord and He heard me, and He delivered me from all my fears." (Psalm 34:4). If that's not healing and victory, I'm still waiting on what is.

ABOUT THE AUTHOR

Ele Momoh currently works as a copywriter. In her spare time, she does other serious things like shopping online. She loves to read, laugh, repeat-watch old movies, and admire beautiful things in life. It is her desire to someday own a modern minimalist home somewhere far away from too many people, where she will write sappy but powerful love stories and afterwards cuddle with her cat and her husband (who is yet to arrive). She loves music and enjoys life.

3

IN ALL THINGS

SOLA MACAULAY

I was watching TV when the call came. I expected the call. What I didn't expect was the content of the call – the kind of news that makes your world cave in. Mum had been battling some unknown illness for a few months and despite all the conflicting diagnoses from different medical quarters, it was unclear what we were dealing with. She's not one who falls ill often so this was new. Fortunately, she had booked a flight to travel to the USA to attend my sister's graduation and had added medical check-up to her itinerary.

The long trip to the US took its toll on her – another new development since she's a veteran traveller. She had lost weight and looked quite gaunt. Mum had always been fleshy and sometimes robust.

The call that came through confirmed a diagnosis I, in my wildest dream, never thought would cross my path. Cancer! I didn't catch the type and I frankly didn't care. Did it matter? Cancer is cancer regardless of where it is eating up the body. That word rocked my world and changed the trajectory of my life. I paced up and down wondering what we would do. The disease spelt death in a lot of cases. Rarely do you see anyone recover from a stage IV cancer. Stage IV is the final stage where all hope is deemed lost. How does a healthy woman suddenly get diagnosed with Stage IV cancer and projected to live no more than eighteen months with chemotherapy and less without chemo? How do you deal with that kind of information? I was shocked, afraid and confused. I had just begun a new phase in my life and things were going quite well. Despite the confusion in my head, I braced up. *After all, I'm a Christian. Ah ah, we will pray that thing off and trust God for complete healing.*

Once she returned from the U.S, my siblings and I met at hers to discuss, plan and pray – though we were all still reeling from the shock of the news. It was hard to accept. I refused to think beyond that moment. I refused to entertain the possibility of death and our favourite Sunday gathering place becoming a distant memory. Whilst concrete decisions were running behind the scenes, we activated a weekly Sunday prayer time at her place. We prayed, petitioned heaven on her behalf and just basked in God's presence. The prayers encouraged and strengthened us for the journey ahead. Sadly, as the prayers grew fervent as the days went by, Mum grew weaker.

We shopped for a local oncologist who administered a low dose drug meant to minimise the growth of the tumours without the damaging effect of Chemotherapy. The drugs provided temporary relief and halted the growth of the tumours but the progress was short-lived. Mum was in constant pain and her visits to the clinic increased in frequency. With these turn of events, it became necessary to strategize.

Hope threatened to slip through my fingers, but I held on to God's word and believed for healing. Yet, I had a nagging sense of death. We needed to be clear on God's will in this situation. Would she, would she not? I daren't hope less yet reality was staring me in the face.

WhatsApp group chat wasn't common then so my siblings and I developed an email chat for our updates on Mum's progress. A decision was made. She wasn't getting better, constantly in pain and with tumours growing back. We sought a second opinion and better medical care. Help came unexpectedly. We secured both a team of medical experts and accommodation, and off to London they went – her and my brother. We established a routine to ensure one of us was always present with her at all times.

My daughter was still little so I didn't get the chance to visit until two months later, in December 2013. But I had to stay at a hotel with my family. A young child with a cold could be infectious and damaging to a grossly compromised immunity.

One day, as I walked to the train station to take my usual ride to visit Mum, God spoke into my spirit these words:
"And we know that all things work together for good to them that love God, to them who are the called according to His purpose."
Romans 8:28

It was a cold yet sunny winter morning and that word lifted my spirit. I knew God was up to something. I knew we would laugh and rejoice at the end. I smiled all the way to Mum's, excited.

While away from the tension and buzz that is Lagos, I took things at a slower pace despite my commute from my hotel to Mum's flat and took time to pray. Not once did I lose my peace. Closer to Christmas, after all the medical tests and all what not, we took her to the clinic for the first round of chemo.

Expectedly, by the next day she was weak. Christmas was in two days. I rushed to purchase some Christmassy food items, snacks and drinks to lighten the mood. That was to be our last Christmas together, but then at the time, I had no idea.

Christmas day lunch was nice but sober. Mum slept all day. By mid-January, we returned to Nigeria. The sister who stayed with her after I did reported she was in high spirits with energy buzzing through her system. Perhaps the drugs had adapted to her body; the news was great. Two weeks later, Mum, still with a burst of energy, visited the mall and played the tourist.

In spite of this great news, many nights I became restless. Deep sleep was rare and visions of us standing around Mum while she lay horizontal bombarded my mind. Optimistically, I'd reason it could mean a recovery visit of some sort. Not once did I entertain death, as that to my mind would be a lack of faith. Does God not heal again?

Then the plan was underway for her to visit Nigeria briefly to see her mum, who had been agitated about her absence. Grandma had been kept in the dark from the true state of things.

You see, my mum was an only child and though she had six of us, she was more like our big sister than our mum. She was a fun loving, down-to-earth and very likeable person. She also had a fantastic relationship with her mother. Travelling back home to Nigeria after her second dose of chemo to visit Grandma became necessary. Deep into January, she arrived home. Unbeknownst to us, pressurisation from air flight worsens the health of people with suppressed immunity. She arrived with her health already tethering on the negative – she could barely stand. On her birthday, which Mum never failed to celebrate – she was big on celebrations – we gathered around her as we joked, laughed and chatted like we always did.

As she watched us, I noticed something flicker across her face and I believe one of my siblings noticed it as well. Her face bore a look of resignation and detachment as though she was hiding a secret from us. As we discussed, I refused to accept the possibilities. I reckoned she was just tired.

When Mum had to return to a local clinic, due to an emergency; our usual prayer was laced with unease because the continuous stream of doctor's reports was grim. One day, she's fine, the next day she's not, and with each report our blood pressure rose and fell.

Despite the deteriorating situation, we never stopped praying, believing and trusting God. There was nothing more the doctors here in Nigeria could do for her. She needed to be flown back to the UK to complete her chemo dose. That was a traumatic moment and a story best told by my brother who took her back to the UK, through many pitfalls of wheelchair and immobility that prevented her from sitting throughout the six-hour flight. The moment they arrived in the UK, things deteriorated rapidly. At this point, I kept reminding myself: "all things would work out for our good". If we lost our mum especially with her aged mother still alive, what would we do?

There was still hope, the medical team said. Surgery was required in order to proceed with the next course of treatment. Once that was done, chemo would resume. At least, we had a fighting chance. We prayed, discussed and looked at the many options before us. I held that word in Romans 8:28 to my chest. *All things must work*. We would testify of God's faithfulness. All would be well.

In early February, my friend and mentor called me and shared her concerns with me. Basically, from her time of prayer, she sensed Mum might not make it. Oh, I refused to believe that. I had my word from God and I was going to hold on to it no matter what. By mid-March, the plan for surgery was cancelled. She was too weak and her immune system had no fighting chance. Surgery equalled death. But we prayed, still.

A week later, sometime around 9 p.m., news came back that all medical treatment had been halted. The cancer had eaten into every part of her body. The medical jargon flew over my head. The bottom-line was she had weeks to live and required only palliative care. There was nothing more the medical team could do. I went to bed but couldn't sleep. I was torn between hope and despair. *Lord, You would still heal her, right?* This was my unasked question deeply embedded in my thoughts. I mean, we've prayed and fasted and confessed and trusted that she would come out of this and testify. What more could we have done? I jumped out of bed in the middle of the night and paced back and forth, praying in tongues and just wanting to hear from Heaven. The next morning, as I took my daughter to school, I felt a wave of darkness sweep over me. It was closing in so fast; like a black hole sucking me into its depths. This strange feeling puzzled me. We detoured to the clinic. Something was wrong and I couldn't place my finger on it. I staggered into the clinic and by the time I climbed on the examining table, numbness spread from my toes to my thighs.

My daughter sat with me, while I grappled with masking the terror I felt inside. When the doctor asked me what was wrong, the usual protocol – I burst into tongues. I was just as clueless, but I sure wasn't going to die. Pricking me once or twice with an injection that bent because my body was stiff, he tried again and again. By this time, the numbness was creeping further up to my tummy region. Fear entered grandiosely, ready to strangle me, but I cried out to God.

As I prayed, the doctor fumbled with a bigger needle and stabbed deep into my stiff thigh. Within a few seconds, warmth seeped into my body and I went limp. I left the hospital a few hours later, unable to decipher the incident but thankful I was alive and well. My siblings had come to join me at home. It was a Monday.

When I attended church on Thursday, God instructed me to give a thanksgiving offering and "let it go". I'd come to accept His instructions without wavering. By evening, I knew Mum wouldn't make it. It's just a knowing I cannot explain. I accepted God's will, albeit reluctantly.

Saturday morning at 2 a.m., my younger sister who was staying with Mum at the hospital called and gave a grim report. I connected the call to another sister and on the conference call, we prayed. That was the least we could do. Maybe our prayers would make a difference. Maybe not, but we prayed. Thirty minutes later, my mum took her last breath and we dropped the phone.

Breaking the news to Grandma, an 89-year-old woman, that her only child was dead, was emotionally draining – filled with its own trauma. We didn't have the luxury to grieve properly as it was an unusual situation. Grieve Mum, yet be strong and comfort Grandma.

My mother was dead. Furthest from my mind was the assurance God gave me in Romans 8:28. I knew it was a bigger concept beyond my plan to twist it into something I found acceptable. Although, it is a comforting scripture yet one I chose not to apply correctly.

God made a way – we had a body to bury and the means to bury her. There were countless testimonies of God's faithfulness throughout the process of bringing her home, tidying up her business and committing her to mother earth.

But I still let some things linger. I had questions. I failed to see the benefit of her death and leaving an aged mother behind. I'd never lost a parent so I was clueless as to how to process the grief. How do I mourn and for how long? Was it okay if I was not happy with God? Was it okay if I needed answers? I felt God betrayed me. You see, God had told me two things to prepare me for my mum's death. 1. He gave me a scripture so I could understand His perspective, (I failed to see that clearly.) 2. During that Thursday church service, He told me to "rejoice". I failed to see what to rejoice over.

But guess what? I ignored all that deep meanings and followed my emotions. I was having nightmares, restlessness, irritability, confusion, unrest, losing weight and eventually fell into depression. I didn't trust God enough to accept His perspective. I didn't trust God enough to accept His definition of "rejoice". I wasn't even sure what I really wanted. God loves my mum, yet her time was up. I didn't love her more than God. I needed to trust God in that decision. I didn't need to understand that.

But depression won and I dragged myself around like I had no God, no purpose. What a sad place to be. When Hubby noticed my psychological malaise, and the fact that I was battling with unknown illnesses, we took a trip to the doctor's who diagnosed depression and placed me on antidepressants. At first the drugs worked fine, and life became light again, until I became addicted. I knew I was in trouble and I hated the idea. The doctor had no alternate plan, rather he warned me, "Don't lose your mind. Cry if you must, but let go." Horrified, my heart skipped too many beats.

Was Yaba left calling my name or what? Ha! Oluwa o!

The doctor turned to Hubby and said, "What your wife needs is a change of scenery, a vacation of sorts." At that point, it didn't sound like such a brilliant idea to me. But the process of jetting out started and within a month, thankfully it was during the holiday, we headed to the airport. Armed with antidepressants, some to help with anxiety attacks on the plane and what not; we left. As I sat on the plane, I contemplated on the past few months. I had become a stranger that I didn't recognise. What happened to that woman who vowed to pray heaven down?

I felt shame wash over me. Who was I? Where was the woman whose only hope was anchored in God? I uttered a heartfelt prayer under my breath, "Lord, help me get through this." The trip was smooth, although I didn't sleep. When we got to our destination, I fell into a deep sleep and woke up with a panic attack. I had never experienced one before. I was alone in the room on the 18th floor with no one close by. I needed to deal with this thing once and for all.

I cried my heart out to God, my emotions a jumble of pleas and rising hope. I asked for physical and emotional healing. In an instant, peace washed over me, the panic attacks halted and I felt God hugging me. All the pent-up anger, pain and overwhelming emotions dissolved. I melted into tears. I was the lost daughter coming back home to her Father. Right afterwards, I chucked all the bags of drugs into the bin. I felt better than I had in months since my mum died. Immediately, God spoke to me and we were back to our usual tete-a-tete. It took a few more weeks of prayer and scriptures, to experience complete healing.

God doesn't always give us answers to our questions, but He expects us to trust Him completely. That was where I dissented. I needed to go back to God and accept His will, His way, His plan in order to fully heal. Through the process of healing, I saw God in a different way.

There is something about the sovereignty of God that some of us don't quite understand. We get all "faith-y" and "spiritual" about certain things to the neglect of God's overall plan and purpose. You see, despite all of Paul's revelations and demonstration of power, the "thorn in the flesh" was something his upper-hand spiritual experience could not unravel. It was a reality he couldn't shake off. It was God's secret, His divine sovereign will.

God doesn't need you to question His sovereign will, but He needs you to 'trust' Him completely. It's okay to ask questions, He is unfazed by our anger, questions and tantrums. But 'trusting' God is for our own good, because He is God who sees all things from all angles, from age to age. We only see and understand what He permits us to see and understand. He is the same God who created the complex cosmos that scientists and astronomers daily study and try to decipher. He placed everything in their place in the entire universe. He thought it all out. Nothing is out of place. Everything fits perfectly. Pray tell me what it is that God cannot handle? What wisdom can we lend God? Do we have an idea what tomorrow will bring, whether we will breathe or not? Yes, God solicits our trust all the time. Read the scriptures; you will find many verses where God says, "Fear not" and "Trust me". His decisions don't have to make sense. Try making an ant understand your words or your world. It is *impossicant*. Pain is unpleasant but it is a gift, when we fully trust God with our pain.

He didn't need to ask us to trust Him but He does so in a gentle way. He wants our complete trust because only God can handle any situation you find yourself in. I know it hurts that you lost someone dear to you. God is not uncaring, but in all things we must rejoice because He knows what we don't know. He has our best interest at heart. He doesn't look at death the way we do. Death for a saint is great gain to heaven. He has never ever failed anyone before and He cannot and will not fail you. It is against His character to do so. In God's hands, *all things work together*. All things. In His time, everything becomes beautiful. Please trust God and trust in God.

ABOUT THE AUTHOR

Sola Macaulay is a lover of God, books, words, long walks, rain, worship, music, art, humour, family and friends. She has a passion for breaking the Word of God down to practicalities, to help people understand, love and embrace God in simple ways. She loves the beautiful things of life and tries to infuse her love of art in everything she does. She's a Professional Editor, Book Coach, Poet, Inspirational Speaker, Author and Publisher.

4

BLESSED WITH A CHILD

KIKELOMO KUPONIYI

A young, newly married woman tends to take many things for granted. I never doubted I would have children, and easily too. In my subconscious mind, I assumed they would come, just like they did for my two sisters. I had helped care for their babies and I just knew mine were around the corner. Neither of my sisters had any difficulty as far as I knew. It was taken for granted.

I got pregnant a month after our wedding and the morning sickness first hit me. Even though I had read about it, I did not expect the discomfort and the accompanying sick feeling. I was not working then, so I was home alone all day. My husband would leave for work incredibly early in the morning and come back late at night, due to the heavy traffic prevalent in the part of Lagos where we lived at the time. We hardly had visitors because everyone dreaded getting stuck in the notorious traffic.

I guess the combination of loneliness and discomfort of early pregnancy affected me. I soon lost a lot of weight and became anaemic. The only food I could eat, that would stay down, was from *bukas*. I could not stand my own cooking. The process was an unpleasant chore because of the different smells created. Everything had a smell. Even water. We agreed I needed a change of environment so I went to stay with my parents.

Two weeks later, I returned home, refreshed and much stronger. My mother had taught me some hacks to deal with the morning sickness and I was coping well. I thought my pregnancy drama was over. And for a while, it was. Around my 20th week, my doctor said it was time to do a foetal scan and I agreed to the procedure. Afterwards, he informed me there might be an issue with the baby, from what he saw on the scan. He recommended I come back with my husband to see the consultant radiologist, who would do another scan. When we did, and the scan was redone, we were told the baby's head had malformed and the pregnancy would not progress. Even if it did, I would give birth to a deformed child that would most likely die. The doctor recommended the baby's evacuation.

I could not believe my ears. We were both shocked and destabilised. This was our first pregnancy. Our first baby! The doctor recommended we go and think about it, but we should not delay, so the situation would not get complicated. We left there very discouraged.

After many tears, my husband suggested we go to our pastor for prayers, but I refused. I told him this was between God and me. Why would God allow my first child to be deformed? Why would God allow this to happen? Why would my first pregnancy be wasted? Looking back now, I know many people have had disappointments with their pregnancies and despite prayer, things did not turn out well. For me, it was just unthinkable. I could not just reconcile or accept it.

I was afraid to show up for my next antenatal appointment because I felt the doctor might just pull the baby out. During the period, I kept away from the hospital. I did not feel sick and the baby kicked normally. But I was still afraid. I did not stop crying out to God. I reminded Him the first child, the opener of the womb, belongs to Him, so whether my baby lives or dies, the child is His. And I wanted my baby to live. I also promised Him I would give the little one to Him wholeheartedly if He would just let my baby live.

The doctor had referred us to a clinic in Yaba, Lagos for a second scan, just to reconfirm what they saw. One day, I summoned up courage to visit. We had been warned I needed to get there early because of the usual long queues. In those days, getting up early to go out was difficult. I still battled morning sickness. I did throughout the pregnancy, but it was milder than the early days. If I followed the dictates of my body, all went well. But if I did not, sickness was just around the corner.

Leaving home early meant not eating. And if I missed a meal, sickness came with a vengeance. I would be nauseous, throwing up and uncomfortable. To cut a long story short, I packaged myself and went for the scan. Although I got there early, there was a long queue already and I joined up. It was hot and inconvenient. I ate the food I had packed and drank some tea (water was a *no no* in the morning).

Eventually, it was my turn. After a brief interview, and a review of my referral note, the lady doctor did the scan. I was overjoyed when she told me afterwards I should not worry. The baby's head was formed and it was developing well. No need to do an evacuation. I was so glad. It was worth all the trouble. With much joy, I reported to my doctor and showed him the scan report. I do not know whether what they saw initially was wrong or whether

God performed a miracle on my baby. What was important was the result had changed. I now had a good report and my baby was okay. My doctor, through subsequent routine scans, later confirmed this. I thought the drama had ended.

The rest of the pregnancy went like a breeze. If I kept to my regular mealtimes, I was okay. Even though the bitter taste in my mouth lasted throughout the pregnancy, and there were some foods I could not eat if I wanted peace, I managed myself. Baby and I were healthy.

On a beautiful Sunday afternoon, I started feeling cramps and since my EDD (Expected Date of Delivery) was close, my husband and I decided to go to the hospital. At that time, even though we lived on the Mainland, our hospital was in Victoria Island. A good friend had highly recommended our doctor and after meeting him, we felt comfortable enlisting at the hospital.

We were well received. I recall the nurse laughing at me when she came and saw me reading newspapers. She said I was not ready, and I just could not understand what she meant. In fact, I was a little irritated with her. Little did I know what was coming.

My labour progressed gradually, and in no time, the newspapers disappeared. I quickly turned into the typical woman in labour, gasping and groaning, and getting angry with my husband, who was there, trying to be supportive and helpful. The labour continued into the night. At some point, my doctor decided I was not progressing and there was an obstruction. He told us he wanted to perform a Caesarean Section to bring the baby out. We both agreed he should go ahead. He left and as far as we were concerned, he had gone to prepare for surgery. About two hours later, I was still moaning and groaning, with no progress. And I was getting tired. I told the nurses to call the doctor. When he came, I told him I could not continue. I was tired. He said he would give me something to relax, because they were not yet ready for the procedure.

The doctor prescribed some drugs, which he said would relax me and help me sleep. That was the beginning of the second level of my suffering. I had been contending with labour pains. Now, the drugs relaxed me. But each time I dozed off, the labour cramps would jolt me awake. It was horrible. And I wanted it to end.

The decision to have a C-section was taken in the early morning hours. However, the anaesthesiologist had been called to come in the morning for the operation. As fate would have it, the next morning was June 13 and it was the first anniversary of MKO Abiola's June 12 event, the cancelled presidential election. Protests had been planned in commemoration of MKO Abiola's struggle. Workers had been warned not to go to work, but to ensure they participated in the protests. Roads were blocked and public transportation was unavailable. To enforce participation of workers, the protest march started early in the morning, with road blockages. As a result, the anaesthesiologist could not make it to the hospital on time.

There I was, alternating between sleep and labour, waiting in pain, agitated. I asked the doctor, "Is this how you're going to leave me and watch me die?" Later, he told me he was so touched by what I said that he decided not to see me again until he brought the anaesthetist to me. That did not happen until around 10 a.m., when the anaesthesiologist eventually arrived, and they were able to proceed with the C-section. To the glory of God, my son survived the stress without any complications and so did I. Till today, I have a friend who refers to my son as "June 12 plus one" baby. That baby is now twenty-six years old.

I cannot take the credit for the outcome of my story. If God had not favoured me and shown me mercy, it would have been a different story. But out of the abundance of His love, He remembered me and had mercy on me. In Mark 11, verse 22, the Bible says, *"Have faith in God."* The subsequent verses 23 and 24 talk about the efficacy of faith as tiny as a mustard seed and praying with faith to receive results. I had faith. I was so sure God was going to give me my baby, alive and well.

My heart was fixed on getting a positive outcome and in all my prayers and cries to God, I kept holding on to the fact that God can and will do it. I refused to even consider the alternative. In times like this, dogged faith is required. Faith that does not consider what is seen but holds on to the promise God has given. Like Abraham who did not consider his advancing years or the ageing of Sarah's body. He remained steadfast in faith and he received God's promise of a child. Yes, he faltered along the line. But he reset his faith and got the promise.

If God has given a promise, He is good enough to fulfil it. He is faithful and His word does not return to Him void. Each word He has spoken is on an errand to fulfilment. Therefore, we can rely on Him and trust Him for our expected outcomes.

On our Christian journey, sometimes, the outcome is contrary to what we desire. However, we still have confidence in God. The confidence that tells us:
- God is Almighty; there is nothing He cannot do.
- Because I have prayed in faith, He has heard me, and He knows what I need.
- I can trust Him to do what is best for me, even when I do not understand what He is doing.
- God loves me unwaveringly and forever. His thoughts towards me are good always. Therefore, I can trust Him.

God is always in charge and in control. He is constantly working out His plans for our individual lives. The plans He put in place before we were ever formed. Nothing pertaining to us is a surprise to Him. He has numbered the hairs of our head. This is because He cares for us and we are precious to Him. Let this be your encouragement.

ABOUT THE AUTHOR

Kike Kuponiyi is a banker, lawyer, and writer. After obtaining her law degree, she ventured into banking and stayed with it for over two decades. Her love for the arts was however retained, through writing journals, poetry, and short stories. She is now retired from banking and is walking with God to navigate His plans for the second half of her life. She is the author of "Unfolding Grace", a Christian fiction novel, which is her first published novel. She blogs at https://kikesthoughts.com She is married with three children and lives in Lagos, Nigeria.

5

GOD IS NEVER INTIMIDATED BY OUR SITUATIONS

DUPE OLORUNJO

I stood shakily in my room that Wednesday morning with a burning fever; my head pounding, my body warning me to lie down and rest, but I knew I shouldn't. I had the opportunity of a lifetime to pursue that day. A once in a lifetime break I knew was from God alone; I couldn't afford to miss it and I couldn't afford to be late. I hardly ever had fevers; hardly ever fell ill, so why did this have to happen at this critical time?

However, the pressure on my body was becoming a strain, my legs threatened not to carry me further, so I decided to lie down for a moment, pray and ask God for strength. As I lay there, my mind wandered a little.

I recalled how I was born into an atmosphere of love – the first of six children with a bonding level close to a hundred per cent. All the ingredients for a happy family abounded – security, contentment, strict discipline, shared stories, and prayer rituals.

Of course, we would fight, but we were not allowed to let the sun go down on our anger. I had a physical fight with my sister once. I was furious and so sure I was not going to speak to her for a long time to come. But then my Dad called a meeting and decreed that because we were siblings, we were not permitted to hold a grudge, bitterness or unforgiveness against each other. We had no choice; we had to abide by his decree of forced sibling harmony. Our parents drilled us on how the sky was the limit and how we could achieve anything we set our hearts to. They also helped us see that with God, everything was possible especially when we had a strong relationship with Him.

My mum, in particular, made sure we understood that the Bible was alive and had the power to regulate all things. I remember what we termed our 'tales by moonlight sessions' when the six of us would sit around, eyes popping and ears attentive, as she shared fascinating stories about the exploits of David, Daniel and Deborah among several other Bible characters. My personal testimony has always been that my mum introduced me to God. It was almost like she said, *Dupe meet God, God meet Dupe*.

My siblings' and my hearts consistently vibrated with the vision of what we could become and so we worked hard and pushed further to excel. We tried our best; passed our exams with flying colours either at the first or the second attempt.

Our home was great. But then very quickly, I had an observation. My parents worked too hard and all they gained was selflessly invested in their children. Their time, their emotions, and every kobo were all redirected to ensure we had a good life. My Dad often worked two jobs and I felt bad seeing him come home late at night, weary and sometimes worn. We had enough for the bare necessities but truly little for any extras.

I remember immediately after my first degree, I decided to go for my MBA. My parents told me it was going to be tough. An MBA is awfully expensive, and they still needed to plan for my younger siblings.

"Why don't you work for a while first and then you can get some money and do your masters?" I shook my head. "No. You guys taught me that the sky is the limit, and an MBA is what I need now." My Dad gave me what he had; it wasn't enough, but at least it was a start.

The next morning, I noticed how the weather was all bright and the sky was clear, promising the possibility of the fulfilment of my dreams. My mum asked me to go with her to the bank. I did and I watched as we stood in front of the bank teller and as she emptied her bank account and handed me all she had.

"That's for you to make up the difference for your tuition fees." My eyes welled up and I pleaded with God in my heart. *Father, please give me the grace to lighten the burden of these two wonderful people. Give me the opportunity to be a blessing to them too.* I prayed hard and trusted that God would make a way.

This was why on that fateful morning, I stood to my feet and made up my mind to leave the house even though I had never felt so weak. I believed God would uphold me and give me the strength to reach my destination. I chartered a taxi. I couldn't risk the possibility of an eventuality that could arise from taking a *molue* or *danfo*, the other more dangerous forms of public transport at the time.

As I sat alone at the back of the taxi, staring at the moving scenery from the window, I remembered how, immediately after I completed my MBA, I started my job search and got three jobs back to back. But the jobs were not really what I was looking for.

They were only stop gaps until I found a job that would not just bless me but also make me a channel of blessing, just like this interview I was going for that fateful Wednesday.

I had applied for this particular job a year before and I sensed God telling me very strongly that the job was mine. But then, I heard nothing from the company. Out of the blue, a letter of invitation for an interview came in a year later and I knew, especially with the passage of time, that this could only be God. Here was an opportunity to step up to the next level, financially, and I made up my mind that no malaria episode was going to stop me.

I arrived at the office building. It was so beautiful, everything I had ever dreamed of. The ambience was top-notch. The staff's professionalism was not like anything I had ever seen, except maybe in movies. At a point, I had to pinch and remind myself that I was not there as a tourist but to be successful at an interview. I was ushered into a room where about thirty other candidates were seated. I sat down and carefully observed them all. They looked fit, strong, and alert.

"How many vacancies does the company want to fill?" I asked the lady sitting beside me and she whispered back, "Three".

My already drooping countenance fell further. I was the second to the last person to be called in. By this time, I had lost it completely. My body ached and my confidence had almost fully seeped out of my mind. I stepped through the door. There were four people on the panel – three men and a lady. I was glad when they asked me to sit as my legs were almost giving way. They introduced themselves. The lady was the head of HR and the others were technical people.

They asked me to tell them a little bit about myself. I was glad; I was able to do that fluently and without missing a word of what I had planned to say. My CV was impressive, and I was happy that they nodded their heads as I spoke.

Then the technical questions started. The man on the far right went first. I didn't hear him, and I politely asked him to repeat himself. He did but I still didn't hear him. I knew it would be foolish for me to ask him to repeat himself again. I tried to answer as best as I could. In between my answers, I counted the members of the interview panel again. *I thought there were four of them but now I counted six*. I was seeing double.

"Lord, please don't let me collapse here," I pleaded in my mind. "That would just be the final straw."

Finally, the interview was over, and the lady spoke up. "I really don't understand what is happening here. You come in with this sparkling CV. You even have an MBA. Yet, your performance at this interview has been very poor."

I looked straight into her eyes and decided to tell the truth. "I've been down with malaria for over a week now, ma, and I am not feeling well at all. I'm dizzy."

"Oh. Ok," said the lady. "I'm really sorry to hear that. I'd like to ask you just one question before you leave."

She asked the question and strangely, I was able to answer it correctly. "Thanks for coming and we will get back to you."

I smiled and left. Outside the building, I started my long walk to the bus stop, and decided to be frank with God. "In recent times, Lord, you have been teaching me about faith. About how I just need to believe you, trust you and know you can do all things. But et me just be honest with you, Lord. At this point in time, I have ero faith that I can ever get this job. I'm sure you know they only eed three out of the thirty people I saw there. And they even told us we're not the only batch they are interviewing. So please Lord, an you help me with another job interview and keep me healthy, o this situation will not repeat itself."

The taxi back home dropped me at my estate gate. Surprisingly, I elt much stronger than I had felt in weeks, so I decided to stop by ur evening estate fellowship. The theme in recent weeks had een about faith. It made sense to stop by and ask God for another job interview and for good health to attend it.

was late so I stepped into the flat and sat close to the entrance. The speaker's voice was loud enough, and I quickly keyed into his words. He asked us to open our Bibles to Romans chapter 4, verse 17. I listened with rapt attention as he read out the passage.

> *17 (As it is written, I have made thee a father of many nations,) before him whom he believed, even God, who quickeneth the dead, and calleth those things, which be not as though they were.*
>
> *18 Who against hope believed in hope, that he might become the father of many nations; according to that which was spoken, so shall thy seed be.*
>
> *19 And being not weak in faith, he considered not his own body now dead, when he was about an hundred years old, neither yet the deadness of Sara's womb:*
>
> *20 He staggered not at the promise of God through unbelief; but was strong in faith, giving glory to God;*

21 And being fully persuaded that, what he had promised, he was able also to perform. (Romans 4:17-21 KJV)

I could not believe my ears. That was God Himself speaking to me directly. I didn't need to listen to what the speaker was saying or his interpretation of the bible passage.

The performance at the interview was dead. My hope of getting the job was dead, just like Sarah's womb and just like Abraham's body. But then because God has told me before that I would get this job, He could still make it possible regardless. God was able to give life to the things that are dead.

Abraham's body was dead. Sarah's womb had already done extra time in the journey of menopause. But Abraham did not consider any of these; he was strong in faith towards God. He was fully persuaded that God could do all He had promised. I could do the same.

My faith revived instantly, my doubts evaporated, and I knew I had this job. For the next two weeks I spoke it and I confessed it. "Thank you, Lord, for this job is mine. Yes Lord, I believe!"

Two weeks later, I got a call for a follow-up interview. About seven of us had been shortlisted. I couldn't stop laughing, couldn't stop dancing and praising God. Can you see how great God is? He is the only One who is able to bring gushing water out of the rock. The One who is able to make a 90-year-old woman conceive. Amazing! I was one of the final three selected and I started work a month later. The salary was ten times more than my job level at the time. Through this experience, God taught me a clear lesson about trusting Him. God is my Father and I am His child. There is nothing in my life that He cannot handle.

And then there was the deep joy I felt about being able to take over some of the responsibilities in the house. I remember how I immediately bought a coloured TV to replace our black and white set. I bought a nice deep freezer, which meant we didn't have to go shopping for foodstuff every other day. I also bought a wall clock and hung it nicely on the wall; we didn't have one before. I gave God all the glory that I could be a blessing to my parents and that He had given me the ability to relieve their burden a little.

A few months later at work, one of the gentlemen on the interview panel walked up to my desk. Even though he was quite senior to me, we had become friends.

"How do you know the head of HR? Are you related?" he asked me. I was puzzled. "No."

'So why then did she fight for you? I mean at the interview?"

'I don't understand," I said.

"When you left the room, she insisted that since you were ill, we should give you another chance. None of us agreed with her, there were so many other good people to choose from. But then she went on and on about how the unexpected happens and how even though you didn't demonstrate capacity, she still believes you should be given another chance."

The story explained a lot. But I know it was really the ability of God to do exceedingly and abundantly more than I can ask or think. My whole life changed due to God's intervention at that interview panel, regardless of how the devil planned for me to fail. As for me, I have learnt to trust Him because if He has promised, He is certainly also able to fulfil His promise.

ABOUT THE AUTHOR

Dupe Olorunjo Dupe is an inspirational fiction writer who loves to create stories to challenge her readers to consider life-changing possibilities sometimes outside their normal reach. She is the author of 4 Novels - Tailed, The Aireginan Dream, A Beautiful Wilderness, and VOICES.

6

DO YOU TRUST ME?

Tope Omotosho

"You aren't going back home. We will have to place you on admission," the doctor said that fateful Friday evening. I looked at him like he had just grown horns. *How am I not going home?* I had never spent the night in a hospital.

In response, my husband told the doctor we wanted to go home to pray. I understood where he was coming from. What the doctor proposed wasn't what we had spent the last couple of months praying and agreeing on. We wanted a natural birth, not C-section.

But no, the doctor didn't agree. He said my husband could go home and pray, but I would have to spend the night. I was numb, struggling to hold back tears. I was scared. I had just visited the hospital earlier that day for a simple antenatal check-up after spending prior hours shopping for baby girl items. *And you say I'm not going home?* I was going to have a surgery. Was the doctor going to pay the hospital bills or what? Did he think we could afford the surgery? I started crying. I really didn't want to have surgery. Yes, my feet were so swollen I had to drag myself from one point of a room to another. But I had assumed that was normal. Also, my blood pressure was 170/90 or so. I didn't understand what it meant at the time. The doctor later explained that I had pre-eclampsia.

I think what really made the news of my reality sink in was when I was told my baby and I could die. My husband didn't have money for surgery, which was three times more than what we would pay for a normal delivery. We were still trying to gather money for the baby's eventual naming ceremony too. I believed God for a natural birth just like the Hebrew women, for a smooth and painless delivery. I now found myself wondering what the point of praying previously was. Was I supposed to keep holding on to what I believed or go with what the doctor's report? Was this God's will for me? What I believed God wanted? Why was I fasting and attending prayer meetings, hoping for a smooth delivery, only to hear C-section?

Eventually, my husband and I obeyed the doctor's orders. My husband went home and returned later with the baby bag we had packed ahead of time. He had a lot of running around to do. Family members kept trooping into the hospital to visit while my blood pressure was monitored. I was given different drugs to keep my blood pressure down. The doctor said he would operate on a Tuesday. That was when the anaesthesiologist would be available.

I really tried to be brave. I kept praying. We even called our pastor who prayed along with us. Come Tuesday morning, my husband had spent two hours plus praying. When he returned, he announced that everything would be okay. That God would take care of us and I shouldn't be afraid. I didn't believe him, but I think ny fear lessened with him by my side in the operating room. I kept praying as much as I could.

When I heard the cry of our baby, I kept reminding my husband to tell the nurses to pierce her ears. My husband just said okay, but why did his face have this look? Later on, he showed me a picture of our child. It was a boy, not the girl we expected! *Ha-ha!* God has a sense of humour. The girl we'd seen while praying was on the way; she just was not arriving then.

From then onwards, my blood pressure gradually returned to normal. God proved Himself faithful. He saw me through the surgery. I didn't need to buy pints of blood. I didn't pass out on the table. Everything was smooth. The doctor was pleased. I was grateful to God for a successful delivery, but my thoughts still lingered on the unexpected expenses. The Bible says, *God shall supply all my needs*. Still, my mind was asking where the money would come from.

You know what? God just did it. I walked out of that hospital debt-free. The way God works? It's beyond comprehension! When God says He will do something, He will. I don't need to question how. I just need to believe.

Shouldn't this experience have taught me to trust in God? To believe His plans and promises for me are good even though they don't go the way I want? I guess just like the Israelites forgot the God who could deliver them from their troubles in the wilderness, I also forgot God would come through for me no matter what. Years later, after giving birth to my second child, who was the girl we saw and believed for just as we saw her, there was another battle to face. Another level of trust to conquer.

I can't eat *roadside food*. I tried roasted plantain and *ponmo* once in high school and have never tried it again since then. I prefer to eat home-cooked meals or buy food from fast-food restaurants knowing I can trust their food preparation. I stick to jollof rice from such joints mostly. If I attempt anything other than that, it's straight to the restroom for me. So whenever I'm out and am offered food, I politely decline. I either tell the host I can't eat or ask for the meal in a take-away pack. If the person asks questions, I tell them I have a weak stomach. And if they insist I eat, I agree.

I've managed this predicament for a long time. I'm even used to my friends and husband making fun of me because of it. Over the years, I've learnt what not to eat and what to eat. I was able to handle myself properly as a Youth Corps member at the NYSC orientation camp by sticking to just jollof rice and noodles.

Then October 2019 happened. When my son was four-months old, he started feeling ill. His tummy was bloated and he kept pooing and vomiting. Like any mother, I was worried, speaking in tongues and surfing the Internet to figure out what was happening in his little body. See me *forming* doctor. I just didn't want another hospital visit. Jesus said by "His stripes we are healed", and I was determined to hold on to this word.

Eventually, my husband and I took my son to the hospital. The doctor's report came in – potassium deficiency. The little one was placed on meds for a few days and got better. Just when we thought all was well, I started having tummy aches. On a particular day, I visited the toilet eleven times. As expected, I became dehydrated. I was later taken to the hospital. My husband never told me I looked pale; the nurses pointed this out with their questions. Even while waiting for the doctor, I visited the toilet frequently. I was immediately given drugs while in the onsulting room and placed on a bag of drip. I'm sure the doctor wondered how I was still standing. At this point, I was tired of the situation and just wanted to go home and sleep. I bluntly declined admission, rejecting the idea of a night at the hospital. Fearful thoughts of people who walk into the hospital and have their corpses wheeled out flooded my mind. Call me paranoid but I was not ready to die yet.

When we arrived home past midnight, I felt slightly better. I even had a good night's rest, but sadly, the recovery was short-lived. I relapsed when I woke up in the morning. That season, I had just finished writing the first draft of my third novel. Coincidentally, it dealt with trusting God. But there I was, struggling to have faith. I couldn't understand what was happening to me. I prayed but I doubt my faith was even up to a mustard seed to believe for healing.

I received my test results from the hospital shortly after. It wasn't bacteria infection, but malaria. Okay. I took the necessary drugs. I visited the hospital daily for injections, but the stooling and occasional vomit didn't stop. I would sleep off during church services because I was too tired and weak. On a particular day, I couldn't stay till the end of service. The children and I had to rush to my mother's house, which wasn't far from my church, so I could vomit and use the toilet in peace, without questions and piteous stares.

During this time, I still had baby fat from giving birth but I lost a lot of it quickly. Sadly, I was still breastfeeding. Also, the food I ate refused to stay down. I was consuming bottles and bottles of Oral Rehydration Salts at home. I even chose the one with an orange flavour specifically (I can laugh about it now but it was far from funny then). Interestingly, my mother-in-law thought I was pregnant (Four months after a second C-section?) but we ruled that out with the earlier test. I eventually had to go for another round of bag of fluid in the hospital. I was so weak that all I could do was sleep.

On a particular day, I spoke to God. I told Him I believed He could heal me. He asked, *Tope, do you trust Me?* I said yes. I couldn't say no. He told me not to answer immediately, but to think about it. I wondered why I had to think about something that already had a straightforward answer. Of course I trusted Him. Again, I told Him I did and He said nothing else. Hours later, my health got better, but went back to square one the following day.

That's when I realised it's easy to say, "I trust You, God" but hard to believe in God for healing and trust His plans are good. My husband tried not to worry during this season; he held the fort by taking care of our children and me. He stood in the gap as an intercessor, crying out to God. Days later, the hospital carried out another round of tests. The results claimed I had typhoid fever. I received treatment but it didn't stop my frequent restroom visits every two or three hours. To complicate matters, I was having ulcer pains. The hospital prescribed another round of medications and these triggered severe back pains. It turned out I had an adverse side effect to one of the drugs.

I struggled to understand why this nightmare of a disease was happening to me. I didn't eat out after all. Was I a victim of a spiritual attack? Had I sinned and not repented? Was the situation a test from God? I must have received at least two to three drips. The doctor didn't sound convinced of his prognosis, offering little assurance. I even had to stop breastfeeding but thankfully, my daughter seemed to understand as she transitioned smoothly to alternatives. I was losing faith, concluding I would lose my life before the end of 2019. But my usband stayed persistent in prayers. While I was weak in my aith, he refused to lose hope in God. He kept pushing in the place of prayer, trusting God for a breakthrough.

stopped visiting the hospital at this point. The doctor had prescribed another round of tests but I was just too exhausted to eceive it. The bills were piling and I wasn't getting better. My conclusion was certain – If God was going to heal me, fine. If not, I had no choice but accept His will. I had reached a stage of resolve - if He didn't heal me, then no one would.

t wasn't long before the illness subsided as quietly as it came. I couldn't eat as much as before by this time; I had to eat in little portions or risk having tummy aches. Minty sweets and chewing gum became my closest companions because they aided digestion.

A year later, I'm still here. Hallelujah! I don't know why I fell ill or what caused the malaria-turned-typhoid. What I do know, however, is God has been so good to me. I am now more confident that He is sovereign and will do what He wants to do. The Bible says in Psalms 9:10 (KJV): ***And they that know thy name will put their trust in thee: for thou, Lord, hast not forsaken them that seek thee.***

Thanks to my experiences, I've learnt that it's easy to sing songs to God and tell Him you trust Him. It's easy to say you have faith that can move mountains but in difficult times and situations, is your faith strong enough to believe and trust Him? Can you trust Him when you don't understand what's happening?

Though He slays me, yet will I trust in him: but I will maintain mine own ways before him. (Job 13:15)

Job held on to God and trusted Him. He lost his children and riches in one day. He developed sores on his skin he had to deal with. Then there was his wife who nagged him to give up on God and die, so she could move on with her life perhaps. Even though Job still believed in God, regardless of his struggles, he still needed one thing – to know why God let it happen. Job queried God, asking why He would allow such calamity happen to him. Just like I queried God, asking why I was suffering. God doesn't always give direct explanations for events in life, but He expects your trust. He expects your dance with Him, that you hold His hand as He guides you lovingly through the trials and tribulations of life because He has already conquered them (John 16:33). As you both dance through the fires and waters with Him leading, as you abandon yourself in His arms.

Brethren, for this reason, in [spite of all] our stress and crushing difficulties we have been filled with comfort and cheer about you [because of] your faith (the leaning of your whole personality on God in complete trust and confidence. **(1 Thessalonians 3:7 AMPC)**

I look back and thank God for His help, even though I still don't know why I had to have a C-section (even after praying) and what caused my illness. I'm thankful to Him for preserving my family from shame; providing my husband and I with all the necessary resources we needed for hospital bills, baby care and naming ceremony. I can also rock jeans I wore four years before marriage – a positive spin from the illness.

I don't need to have all the answers. I don't need to be afraid when He says I should trust Him even though I don't have my miracle, or things aren't going the way I think they should. I can trust that He works everything for my good (like He did with my health and delivery scares). I can trust Him because He's always good. Always true. Always faithful. He is a God that can always be trusted regardless of my present circumstances and I pray for grace to keep trusting Him.

ABOUT THE AUTHOR

Tope Omotosho is a believer in Jesus Christ and writes His heart and is interested in pleasing Him first. She is a wife and mother of two. She's an author and is passionate about impacting the world through her thought-provoking stories. Her stories and articles cut across love, relationship and romance in a way that does not deny the relevance of God in our everyday life. She is passionate about bringing people to the knowledge of God's true and unfailing love.

7

LEAN NOT ON YOUR OWN UNDERSTANDING

ADAH DOEBELE

"It is time for your book!" I smiled because I did not understand it.

My book? I repeated in my ignorance, as if to prompt the Holy Spirit to explain further. *Who am I to write a book?* I wondered aloud. *I am nothing, just a high school leaver with an average performance.* I had lived my entire life severely wounded, believing I was possibly the ugliest woman on earth. I was scalded in all areas of my being – spiritually, physically and emotionally. I was in complete bondage based on what had been repeated to me hundreds of times since my childhood.

I woke up and went on with my morning as if nothing had happened, not knowing that Monday would be the beginning of the rest of my life. It was the 20th of April 2014 to be exact.

After having my breakfast that fateful morning, I grabbed my Ipad, a device fondly received from my son as a gift. By the time I placed the device back on the table, I had written sixty pages of

Adornment One through sobs, flowing tears, pain and other emotions apparently bottled inside me.

I first met God six years earlier in an unimaginable, life-changing encounter. For months, my two oldest children had been nagging me to accept His son, Jesus Christ, as my Saviour. *They do not understand how messed up my life is*, I would reason. *Would God even have me?*

I grew up knowing about God, but my limited knowledge of Him as my Father would not let me seek after His heart. I was convinced I had messed up my life, by first being married off at fifteen years of age to a married man, who I later walked out on at the age of twenty-one. The bold move was due to excessive mental, physical, emotional and any other abuse thinkable he and his first wife inflicted. He battered my person to the point I was thoroughly ashamed of myself and apologetic to people for being a human being.

Little did I know God loved me regardless, abundantly and unconditionally. At some point in February 2008, with only ten Kenyan Shillings to my name and no idea where my children's next meals would come from, I finally surrendered my struggles to God and told Him so. Unknown to me, that act was exactly what He was waiting for.

The Lord took my case up instantly and He then worked in my life so fast, my head spun. He led me to an anointed pastor, gave me the desire to seek Him with all I am, healed my son of asthma and sent him to the United States to study within a span of three months. These testimonies totally transformed my life. A domino effect indeed! I continued to seek Him passionately.

Fast forward to the present and He was now instructing me to write the story of my life in a book with the title *Adornment* which apparently is the meaning of my name, Adah, in Hebrew. When the Lord healed my son of asthma, I desired to fully trust and remain in obedience to Him. This was the beginning of my spiritual growth journey. I would later get the understanding that God created me fearfully and wonderfully, and that I can do anything through Christ who is my strength. He would later anoint me audibly as I sat under an acacia tree on a stone. He directed me to an encounter that left me completely broken and humbled in total submission. He commissioned me to witness for Him in Truth, through Adornment Ministries, which He said is a ministry of healing. With it, He gave me verses in Isaiah 61:1-3: *The spirit of the Sovereign LORD is on me, because the LORD has anointed me to proclaim good news to the poor. He has sent me to bind up the broken hearted, to proclaim freedom from the captives and release from darkness the Prisoners, to proclaim the year of the LORD's favour and the day of vengeance of our God, to comfort all who mourn, and provide for those who grieve in Zion—to bestow on them a crown of beauty instead of ashes, the oil of joy instead of mourning, and a garment of praise instead of a spirit of despair. They will be called oaks of righteousness, a planting of the LORD for the display of His splendour.*

Having suffered so much abuse from both relationships I walked away from, I could not even find me in the mirror. This lack of self-esteem prompted me to respond negatively to God's call on my life. He said to me, "My Spirit is upon you and I am with you." I answered, "Lord, this is Adah. Your Adah, the nothing!"

He repeated His sentence. I had embraced people's opinions of me and never thought He could use me as His vessel. I had written myself off and knew the only thing I could do in church was manual service like cleaning.

The Lord continues to do great things in my life. Since 2019, He has given me songs. Singing is something I thought I could not do. It is most humbling and my desire to be transformed into His likeness is ongoing.

It does not matter where you may be or what another person's opinion is of you. God knows what He created you for, therefore, "Seek ye first the Kingdom of God and His righteousness, and all these things shall be added to you." These things include wisdom, knowledge, understanding, and discernment - things which hold keys to right living. The scriptures tell us in Romans 12:1-2: *Therefore, I urge you, brothers and sisters, in view of God's mercy, to offer your bodies as a living sacrifice, holy and pleasing to God—this is your true and proper worship. Do not conform to the patterns of this world, but be transformed by the renewing of your mind. Then you will be able to test and approve what God's will is—His good, pleasing and perfect will.*

God is faithful and able! Within the span of a year, my three children were studying abroad despite my lack of a job or business. I had God, the creator of the universe and everything in it. Let God be God!

Doubt would creep into my mind often, if indeed He called me. He then gave me a deep desire to attend Bible studies, enabling me to join in the middle of an ongoing study, which was quite unusual. Participants were studying the life of Moses. I eventually learnt the Bible hero had similar thoughts like I did. He did not think he was worthy to serve God and offered excuses about his speech and demeanour. We know, after being reassured by God, he went on to fulfil a great mandate under God's protection and guidance.

I would never have thought that God would restore me to wholeness and even bless me with a wonderful husband even with my messy past, but He did. Yes! We can do anything through Christ who strengthens us, for He who promised us is faithful and able.

ABOUT THE AUTHOR
Adah Doebele is married to a wonderful man and blessed with seven wonderful Children, and one granddaughter. Her most important undertaking is my spiritual journey towards getting close to GOD. She writes spiritual inspirational books and preaches in Church at women's gatherings and conferences.

8

HOPE THAT DOESN'T INTIMIDATE!

YVONNE EBBI

I paced the room a dozen times. I was not saying anything audibly. Instead, my heart was having the conversation. I had learnt to have normal conversations with Divinity. We had that type of relationship. He was my Father and that was my understanding of our relationship. I talked, argued, thanked and sometimes, attempted to advise Him.

This cheeky child!

I knew that He loved me. I was not afraid to make mistakes. If I was rude or wrong, He would correct me. He is my Father, see?

I continued the conversation audibly:

"Lord," I said. Trying to put my conversation in context, I continued, "Nné is not ready for a family yet..."
"You know that they got married a few months ago, yes?"
"Ehen..."
"She wants to settle down and sort out the financial crises rocking

their home."

"She's my friend and she explained her plight to me."

"But, me?"

"I am ready, Lord."

"Like, ready."

"So, how did you mix up the prayer points?"

"You are God – Almighty. All Knowing. Immortal. Sovereign!"

"So, how did this happen, Lord? How?"

"Lord, she just found out she was pregnant and she's miserable about it."

"She's heart broken."

"Her husband just got admission into school and the whole weight of managing the home is on her."

"Now this?"

"I want to be pregnant and nothing is happening."

"I'll ask again."

"Did you mix up the prayer points, Lord?"

I was still pacing as I asked. I glanced at the home pregnancy test result, again. It was clearly negative. My mind strayed. Surely these home tests have a factory defect, I mused, or how else would you explain having a negative result every single month? Then, I stopped and said:

"Wait, Lord..."

"Wait a minute!"

"Oh no..."

"No, no, no..."

"Let's get this straight..."

"Oh my God!"

"We said we didn't want a honeymoon baby..."

"True."

"I remember that."

"But, I also said I wanted to wait for three months, max..."

"Three months, Lord."

"One, two, three."
"Three like, 3.'
The third number.
"The number after 2."
"Numeric 3."
"The digit, 3."
"1, 2, 3...!!!!"
"Oh, Lord!"
"When I said three months.... I meant three biological months. Like July, August, September. I realise that a day with you, Lord, is like a thousand years. But, I wasn't talking spiritual, Lord! I meant 3 human months o."
"Three months, not three years!"
"Time is far spent, Lord!"

And I began to advise Divinity on how it was important to give me a child. "Lord," I continued, "There's no problem bigger than you. And there's even no problem, *sef.*"
"Lord, do you remember Mary? Mary, your earthly mother? Mary did not even know a man and yet she got pregnant. Lord, think about that. The Bible tells us that she did not know a man. Yet, she got pregnant solely by divine intervention."
"Lord, I've gone ahead of Mary."
"I know a man, Lord..."
Then, I knelt down and just asked God to help me. I often wondered what God thought about me. Maybe, He said something like, "Jesus, your drama queen has come again!"

Even though I greatly desired a child, I wasn't obsessed by the desire. Apart from the conversations with God, I lived a normal life. Deep inside, I believed God would eventually grant my heart's wish. I prayed and waited.

Being a Christian before I was ten years old, and having

experienced God's deliverance from all kinds of crises, I knew He would come through at the appointed time. He makes all things beautiful in His time. He who began a good work in me would be faithful to complete it.

Another incident made me smile. A friend of mine, Anne, had a situation. A paradoxical situation. Anne and I got married about the same time. Actually, we got married on the same day. And like me, she wanted to have a brief season to enjoy her husband and her new home. She was certainly not in a hurry to have children. Then, it happened. She had two children in quick succession. This was hardly what she expected. In the space of two years, she had two toddlers. *Phew!*

A handful. She was grateful but clearly flustered. She worked in a multinational company and had hopes of building her career and climbing the corporate ladder. Now this? Everything was happening with such speed. She wondered how she would recover. She returned to work after her second maternity leave and was thankful her mother was around to help. A few weeks after resumption, Anne discovered she was expecting her third child. I met her shortly after she found out she was pregnant and she just broke down in tears while we talked. She was already a new wife and mother of two under 2s. How was she going to cope? I found myself comforting her. Anne wanted what I had. I desired what she had. Life! I smiled as I cheered her up. In that moment, I realised there wasn't an issue of scarcity of children. My babies were safe in God's custody and would be in my arms at the appointed time. I was assured that as He had promised; He would perfect all that concerned me.

I remembered Sarah in the Bible and Paul's account of her in the book of Hebrews. *"Through faith also Sara herself received strength to conceive seed, and was delivered of a child when she was past age..."*

Her testimony had always encouraged me. I had learnt the paragraph by heart and often confessed it. That day, however, I read the verse and received divine illumination. The last phrase was very insightful.

"Through faith also Sara herself received strength to conceive seed, and was delivered of a child when she was past age, BECAUSE SHE JUDGED HIM FAITHFUL WHO HAD PROMISED." Hebrews 11:11 [emphasis added]

That was a whole new level for me. A whole new vibe! Because she judged Him faithful. She judged Him faithful. She believed. She believed in the One who was able to bring her heart's desires to pass. My faith level went a notch higher.

I also loved the story of Hannah. I enjoyed Samuel's account of her situation and read it over and over. One day, as I read her story, something popped out of the pages. Light. Insight. Illumination. That's the beautiful thing about the word of God. It is a living word. Read it a hundred times, and you'll still find something new. The Bible says: *"For the word of God is quick, and powerful, and sharper than any two-edged sword, piercing even to the dividing asunder of soul and spirit and of the joints and marrow and is a discerner of the thoughts and intents of the heart."*

Hannah desired to have a son after many years of barrenness. She prayed her heart out after making a vow to God. As she prayed, she spoke in her heart; only her lips moved, but her voice was not heard. Therefore, Eli thought she had been drunk. Eli rebuked her when he said, *"How long wilt thou be drunken? Put away thy wine from thee."*

Hannah's response was calm. *"No, my lord, I am a woman of sorrowful spirit: I have drunk neither wine nor strong drink, but have poured out my soul before the LORD. Count not thine handmaid for a daughter of Belial: for out of the abundance of my complaint and grief have I spoken hitherto*

Then Eli answered said, *"Go in peace: and the God of Israel grants thee thy petition that thou has asked of him."* Reading this story for the umpteenth time revealed Hannah's armour of faith.
It is true tears are not enough.
It is true it is impossible to please God without faith.
It is true the just shall live by her faith!

I often wondered how Hannah's faith was measured until I read the eighteenth chapter of 1st Samuel. Faith is a deliberate action. A verse says concerning faith: *"Faith is the substance of things hoped for, the evidence of things not seen."* (Hebrews 11:1)

Hannah believed God. How can we prove that Hannah believed God? Is there a *faith-o-metre?* How do you measure faith? How do we know for certain Hannah had faith, believed God and trusted Him? This is how we know: And Hannah said, *"Let thine handmaid find grace in thy sight."*

What was Hannah's action of faith? What did she do? *So the woman went her way, and did eat.* She went her way. And did eat. And her countenance was no more sad. Light bulb moment!

Joy is a product of faith. Happiness happens when we fully trust God. The Bible says, *"Therefore, with joy shall ye draw water out of the wells of salvation."* (Isaiah 12:3)

My disposition is directly proportional to my faith! That was a divine revelation that kept me as I waited for the fruit of the

womb. I praised, regardless. I laughed. I lived. I loved.
I had fun.
I danced.
I played.

I prayed, believing. Sometimes, I cried, as I prayed. Sometimes I got overwhelmed and wept. But, joy welled up within afterwards. I rejoiced in the present, knowing my future was in the hands of the One who had a track record. I played. I cheered others. Children are a heritage of the Lord and the fruit of the womb is His reward. End of discussion!

In 2004, my husband and I joined a foreign missionary group for a medical missionary expedition. Ten days later, we returned home. It was a beautiful and fulfilling outing. Lives were changed. Souls were saved. Spirits were rebirthed. We relished the experience as we settled in. Soon enough, I felt slightly off. A bit poorly. So, I went to see the doctor.

The problem was detected and I picked up my medication from the pharmacy. Malaria parasite. What nerve? Just before leaving the hospital, I quickly mentioned to the doctor that it had been three years and yes, we'd been trying. He took my history and did a physical examination.

"There's no reason why not," he said. "Everything seems good. But let me see you both after your next cycle. We'll run some tests."
"And one more thing," he added. "Don't do the needful!"
"Why doctor?" I enquired.

He briefly explained that x-rays could have adverse effects on the foetus. For some reason, that simple explanation gave me hope. So, he did see a possibility of a foetus? Really? I was excited.

When I got home, I shared the day's experience with Hubby. Every bit of it. No detail was left out. We were both eager and expectant for the possibilities that lay ahead. Weeks later, in our little, cosy home, before we were scheduled for our medical appointment, the room was cold. The kind of cold that needs human intervention. The duvet didn't suffice. The blanket couldn't deal. The cold brought two warm hearts together. An emotional paradox. Friendship ignited fellowship. Oh, the joy, the bliss, the ecstasy. The heat of passion! Half mesmerized, I reminded Hubby about the caveat.

"We really shouldn't. Our appointment is..."

I didn't finish the sentence for I knew we had both reached the point of no return. We had crossed the Rubicon and had to complete a divine task. Oh, the craft. The mastery. Pure bliss! The doctor's appointment would have to wait. Surely, there'll be a next time. So, we did the needful even though we shouldn't have. And that was it. A simultaneous solution to a quadratic equation: Y found X and the journey began. Unbeknown to us, we would later realize the seed had been planted.

The uterus had welcomed a bundle of blessings. Oh, the joy! The rest, as they say, is history. Needless to say, I didn't make the doctor's appointment. I was busy dealing with nausea and weird cravings and reading books like *What to Expect When You're Expecting*.

On May 16th 2005, our son popped out. He weighed a whooping 3.2 kilograms. A clear bundle of blessings – a timely gift. We named him Bryan Ikechukwu – a symbol of strength. A testimony indeed and a beautiful blessing. Today, we celebrate the outcome as we remember the Faithfulness of God. We're extremely thankful that we did the needful.

ABOUT THE AUTHOR

Yvonne Ebbi is an Oxford alum, TEDx Speaker and a Social Intelligence expert with specialty in corporate image branding, personal branding, executive presence and business etiquette. She is the Lead consultant of The Etiquette Place, a corporate finishing school changing the narrative in matters of executive intelligence, work ethics, best practice and proper public conduct.

9

LETTING GO AND LETTING GOD

MARY UMOH

I find it simply amazing how the Lord God Almighty takes us through times and seasons of trials when we must trust in His ability to see us through. When I think back to such seasons of many years ago, I realise that trusting Him was the only way to go. I'm still standing still and letting God do His thing is. Well, let's rewind to twenty-five years ago in 1995.

Young, upcoming career lady working in the oil & gas sector. Up north, Kaduna. Life was simple, so it seemed. The only things I lacked were a car, an air conditioner, a generator and a microwave oven. Light was constant and I lived near my place of work, so why spend on what I could comfortably live without?

"I advise you go check this thing on your neck," Sam, my colleague, told me, one day. "What?" I retorted, rather irritably.

He, Sam, had just committed the heinous crime of disrupting my beautiful session while taking in the icy blast of the split unit air conditioner installed in the laboratory recently.

"Okay Sam, I'll check it out."

I had, for several months, noticed a few unexplainable changes in my body. When I arrived at home, after sorting out stomach infrastructure, I settled down in my parlour. With two mirrors in my hand, I tilted them at angles so I could manoeuvre to see my profile perfectly, or even the back of my head. My eyes widened as I noticed the swell on the lower end of my throat. A lump. I swallowed and watched as it rose gently and settled back to rest at the base of my throat. It made me look like a resting camel. Come to think of it, it reminded me of a smooth version of a turkey's neck waddle. I watched as the lump rose and fell as I swallowed, and I was totally dismayed. *Yuck!* A whole babe like me with a lumpy neck. *Ha!*

I sat down heavily, examining this lump – this thing that totally marred my considerably good profile. My eyes looked funny too. Bulging.

"Something must be wrong," I told myself, suddenly emotional. "What could it be?" I asked no one as tears rolled down my eyes.

That night, I fell asleep after enjoying a tub of creamy yoghurt as my final nightcap. And the evening and following morning marked the first day of my adventure into this discovery.

Fast-forward to 2000. I was sitting in the office of Port-Harcourt Teaching Hospital's chief radiologist with an ultrasound probe on my abdomen. After a scan, he told me I have fibroids. I looked at him and before I could ask any more questions, in walked this tall, stern but beautiful, middle-aged Indian lady, complete in her lovely sari outfit. A red beauty spot in the middle of the forehead and adorned in simple but beautiful jewellery. She exchanged pleasantries with my radiologist and locked eyes on the screen, then looked at me. *"Young lady, you ah considering having children, right? Vit da hyperthyroid, you cannot conceive and even if you do, da fibroids in your voomb vill not allow da baby to stay. There is absolutely no space in thiaah at all. Your voomb valls are totally closed in. You vill have to take kiaah of dem both surgically if you expect yany-thing at all."*

What? Ha! To say, I was stunned is an understatement. I dressed up and went home in a daze. I refused to attend my midweek fellowship with my husband of about ten months. I stayed at home all alone and had a good old *pow-wow* with my heavenly Father. After all, I had no juju man, prayer house, native doctor, oracle, talisman, ancestral shrine or whatever people consult on such critical issues. I knew I was on a path that would be difficult. This I knew when I had no clear word on whether to go ahead with surgery and just trust in Him to do what He felt was best. I literally begged the Lord, "Please Father, I don't need that great testimony of waiting so long before I have children. Please make conception normal for me." I had yet another mountain to climb, walk around or blast through.

I washed my face and braced myself for the wait. I wondered why mosquitoes had to exist and why God hung the planets in outer space; it all seemed unfair to me in the light of my plight. Then His word came, saying I was His chosen beloved daughter who Christ died for, and there would be none barren in the land. I could only wait and trust He would do something good, though I didn't understand the path I had to walk.

Prior to this, five years earlier in Kaduna, my visit to the doctor revealed my thyroid gland was overactive. In other words, my thyroid gland was still over-secreting thyroxin, the thyroid hormone responsible for metabolism in the body and control of virtually every other internal function. My fingers and palms trembled always. I had mastered the art of masking sensations with sunglasses and controlled hand movements.

The thyroid gland is the little engine box of the human body. It controls brain function, reproduction, temperature tolerance and regulation, mood, emotions, metabolism, weight gain and loss, appearance and pretty much every other function in the body. That little bow-tie shaped organ situated at the throat's front-base, near the voice box, has that much power. My hormone levels went through the roof and my pulse rate was steadily between 140 and 160 instead of 75 and 80. I was placed on a daily prescription of 45mg TDS. Carbimazole (to increase the heart rate) and 40mg Inderal, a beta-blocker (to help regulate my heart) for the next twelve years. The palpitations gave me heart problems.

Letting go and letting God is much easier said than done. Having to buy sanitary towels monthly when you're looking forward to the fruit of the womb while waiting to hear a word from the Lord, and knowing you cannot afford to seek "help" from any other source, can really fray the nerves. So I simply shut down my emotions, ready to trust Him one day at a time, anticipating a very long wait.

Within two months, I found myself pregnant. Hyperthyroid and fibroids were still firmly in place. Contrary to the medical reports, and miraculously, the thyroid hormones didn't hinder conception. The fibroids gave way and allowed the baby to grow. Talk about the parting of the Red sea. By the 36th week, I delivered a beautiful baby girl by natural birth. I had two more babies all within the space of four years with all these medical issues still present. It was just an awesome manifestation of God's response to trusting Him. He simply did it. He has never failed me yet.

The Bible has stories of several people with issues beyond the sufferers' capabilities. These individuals had situations that would lead to hopelessness. However, we see them pressing on. I can't help but mention more than one example because I draw so much strength from these stories and relate them to my life. Can we remember the Syrophoenecian woman with the sick son (Mathew 15:22-28), the Centurion with the sick servant (Luke 7:2-10), the woman with the issue of blood (Luke 8:43-48), the four friends with their friend sick with the palsy, Naaman the leper... the list is endless.

They all physically had no hope but trusted that if they went to the Lord, He would help them. I had a medical certification of what could never be considered normal. Even my gynaecologist was sceptical. My first pregnancy was rather traumatic and extreme medical interventions were recommended so my life would be saved. Through it all, the Lord spoke to me and held my hand. I only received extra hydration and bed-rest and trusted Him to take care of me. He proved that He's indeed able to do exceedingly abundantly above what we ask or even imagine.

ABOUT THE AUTHOR
Mary Umoh is a graduate of Applied Chemistry. She worked as the Quality Assurance Coordinator in the production chemistry laboratories and has handled training programs for SUBEB Akwa Ibom and Rivers States. She is currently pursuing a doctorate in Special Education from the Ignatius Ajuru University of Education, Port Harcourt.

She is married with four beautiful children.

10

THE CERTAINTY OF TRUST

DR. ANGIE TOLUHI

In the *The Hand You Hold*, I narrated how God led me to study Medicine and how He proved Himself faithful throughout my academics. Well, in 2019, I decided to embark on another journey of faith with the Father.

After graduation from Med school, I went through internship and then left for NYSC in the South-eastern part of Nigeria. I was posted to a local government HQ Clinic. I volunteered for a faith-based NGO that specialised in providing free medical outreaches in underserved communities across Africa. I would later work for this organization. This is the backdrop against which my passion for community medicine and public health was born.

After my NYSC, I joined the faith-based organization I had mentioned earlier as a Volunteer Primary Care Physician for six months under their Medical Volunteers Program (MVP). The name of the organization is Pro-health International (PHI). We travelled within Nigeria and Africa, providing short-term medical and surgical care to poor and underserved communities. I later worked in the Head Abuja Office of this organization. Thereafter, I moved on to development work and worked with several international NGOs. For more than fifteen years, I worked in Nigerian and African communities to develop and promote health interventions. I developed a strong professional interest in infectious diseases, health systems strengthening, maternal and child health, adolescent health and nutrition.

It was while working with PHI that I first used the local cereal-soy-groundnut blend to manage a case of moderate malnutrition. I would go on to champion many initiatives to improve the health of mothers and children in Nigeria through the organizations I worked with. In September 2018, while working for an international NGO which specialised in health, agriculture and emergency/humanitarian services, I was asked to move to Ghana for three months to help them start up a maternal and child health project. I was happy to do this and threw myself into the work there. While I was in Ghana, God began to bring back to my memory certain visions and dreams He had shown me while I was in medical school. One of those visions involved work in the US. I had been traveling to the country and UK for holidays as well as to take some training courses.

I had not tried to relocate too much. Several years before, I had been denied a student visa and so had closed that chapter and only travelled for pleasure or professional purposes. In any case, God began to quicken this desire in me. He also sent a friend who began to push me to apply for my doctoral degree. We had shared along this line in the past and she had begun her applications. For some reason, she felt she had to be on my case to get my applications in. I thank God for her, because without her prodding, I probably would not have done it. So, I applied to three universities in the US and continued my work. Between March and May 2019, I received admission offers and had to decide which to accept. One thing was clear to me: even if I saved all my money for the next only-God-knows number of years, I would not be able to finance my academics. Furthermore, I am averse to taking loans or borrowing money. So, the first thing I did was go to my Abba Father and tell Him the exact situation of things (as if He didn't know already). I told Him that except He provides the funds, I couldn't fund this project.

To many people, it didn't make any sense that I would leave a very good job to go back to school. You see, I had risen to a senior management level in the international development space. Because of the good remuneration at this level, it is quite uncommon for people to just pack up and go back to school with no assurances of funding support. Even my Dad did not think it was such a good idea. In fact, some people close to me felt I had reached the stage where I could start my own NGO. Yet, here I was talking about going back to school. It didn't make sense. So, I "explained" the situation to God and asked Him how to proceed. Like Moses, I more or less told Him to leave me where I was if He was not going to go with me. I felt Him say to my spirit, "go" and 2 Corinthians 9:8 came to my spirit and mind as the rhema word for this situation.

Well, I finally accepted the offer for the University of Alabama at Birmingham (UAB) in Birmingham, Alabama US. Then I began the process of getting ready to resume school and raising the necessary funds. I was able to raise some money from my savings, the sales of my car and some other possessions. Friends and family also supported, as they knew how. During this time, I underwent two major surgeries and was still recuperating by the time I went for my student visa interview. I was issued my visa without any problem and so I promptly resigned my position with my organisation.

I think it was at this point that the gravity of my actions began to dawn on me. My job represented security. Going for my doctoral studies was uncertainty. Yet, I knew this was what God wanted me to do. With faith in my heart and questions in my head, I left Nigeria five weeks after my second major surgery. So many things began to shake my faith when I arrived at school. For one, I had not been able to secure accommodation before leaving Nigeria. I had been discouraged from going for the school's student housing by friends who had schooled in the US. To sign a lease, I was asked to get a co-signer resident in Alabama. How was I going to do that? I had no relative in the state. God stepped in; through a friend; someone who did not know me co-signed a lease for me. If you know anything about living in the US, you will know that it could only have been God. It took me two weeks of spending money on Airbnb rental home, before I was able to sign a lease for an apartment.

Although I was still healing, Fall semester went well for me per studies. I then began to source for funding for school. By God's arrangement, I connected with the Director of International Fellowships and Scholarships in the school. We hit it off instantly and she was very impressed with the work I had done prior to coming to UAB. With her help, I sent in several scholarship and fellowship applications. However, none of them would send responses until the next year 2020. Over the Christmas break, I spent time waiting on God and talking to him about my dwindling savings, reminding him of His promise to me in 2 Corinthians 9:8. During this time, God led me to start a blog to encourage ladies and young Christians to read their Bibles by sharing Bible stories through a modern lens. The blog is called *Conversations with Abba* because it was borne out of my conversations with my Abba

Father during this time. God also showed how to live a life of continuous worship, which birthed a new level of joy in my life.

During this time, I also met with the head of my department and she promised to help work something out by the first week in January. With that assurance from the HoD, I was able to enjoy my Christmas break and focus on starting the New Year on a strong note. However, by the second week in January, I still hadn't heard from my HoD. I began to have some conversations with myself on what my next steps would be if I did not get funding support. I then began to send out applications for international health development work. To her credit, my HoD came through for me with a Teaching Assistant job by the end of January. However, since it did not cover my tuition, it really was not a sustainable funding support. By February, I was pleasantly surprised by a travel scholarship from my department for a research proposal I had submitted. It still did not cover my tuition. I pressed on with my job search.

By March, CoVID-19 had forced everyone into a lockdown and I had received two rejection letters from two of the most promising scholarship applications. I still believed God but I also needed to be realistic. I was contacted by several of the places I applied to jobs. However, the most promising one wanted me to resume almost immediately. This was not possible and so I lost that opportunity. It was like everything was going awry but as I wrote earlier, God had been teaching me about living a life of worship unto Him. The more I worshipped God, the more He infused my spirit with joy, grace and strength to keep trusting. A fellow African doctoral student and I had applied for the American Association of University Women's (AAUW) International Fellowship. She was also trusting for funding support.

When we submitted our applications for the AAUW fellowship, we were informed that the results would be out by the third week in April. By the 14th of April, the African lady had received a rejection letter from AAUW and called me to ask if I had heard from them. I hadn't. We agreed to keep praying. The director who had helped with my applications sent a mail to ask me about the status of my application on the same day. I refused to answer her mail. I did not want to dampen what little faith I had left. By this time, worship had become the air I breathed. I just began to worship Him. I did that overnight. I remember waking up on the morning of April 15th, about to start thinking of funding issues again. I reached for my phone and saw a mail had come in from the AAUW. I was a little scared of opening it because of my friend's report the previous day but I steeled myself. As I opened it and saw the first word, I just dropped the phone and began to thank God. All I saw was "Congratulations!" I lay on the floor and just worshipped.

The names of God that came to me were "Oro'mo n'ise f'aya ti" and "A to farati bi oke". I was so relieved. It was like a large load had been rolled off me. I had enough to cover my tuition for the next year. I forwarded the mail to the director. Before I knew it, the President and Vice President of the university, and other senior officials of the school, began to send me congratulatory messages. One of my professors sent a mail calling me "a star". I was interviewed for the school's news platform. God turned it around, but He wasn't done. Other doors began to open, and God has just been proving Himself faithful and worthy of being trusted. Remember my African friend? She also secured a scholarship from one of the organizations she applied to. God is awesome and His goodness extends to all His children.

As I wrote above, when I think of this episode of my life, the part of the Bible that resonates most is the story of Moses and the exodus of the children of Israel in Exodus 33:12-19. I knew that unless God went with me and provided for me, this vision was not sustainable. But because He has been with me, I have never lacked. Beyond this funding, God has met my needs in so many other ways. It has been a mind-boggling experience. Sometimes, I just tell God He spoils me too much. People here look at my life and are encouraged at how God has distinguished me. I give Him alone all the glory. Like when I went to ABU for my medical studies, I had no guarantees; only the Word God gave me. This has been the hallmark of my relationship with the Father. When things look impossible and there seems to be no way out, I know if I can just get a word from Him, everything will be alright. The way to get that word is to worship and be still. Psalm.46: 10. Like in the case of Elijah in 1Kings 19:11-13, God will not usually come in the wind and fire but in the still small voice. When it looks like it's not going to happen, hold on to the rhema word He gave you. He can NEVER lie. Even if the opposite is happening, trust Him. He will not fail you. He has never failed me.

ABOUT THE AUTHOR

Dr Angie Toluhi is a development and public health professional with several technical competencies including public health, nutrition, maternal and child health, HIV programming and development program management. She holds a medical degree from the Ahmadu Bello University as well as a master's degree in Public Health (Global Health) from the University of Manchester,

---

4. *His job is to take care of me.*
5. *The dependable God*
6. **Psalm 46: 10** *He says, "Be still, and know that I am God;*
I will be exalted among the nations,
I will be exalted in the earth."

UK. She is currently a doctoral student at the University of Alabama at Birmingham (UAB), USA where she is pursuing a Doctor of Public Health degree in the Maternal and Child Health concentration.

11

GOD HAS DONE WELL

GOZIE UDEMEZUE

I got married to an excellent man. With him, I had all I could ever ask for: vacations abroad, a beautiful daughter who was born a few weeks after we got married, a beautiful home, domestic staff at my beck and call, and enough support to enable my schooling – I was studying Law at the time. What on earth did I need salvation for?

Two years after the birth of my daughter, I started to worry when I realised my husband and I were struggling to conceive again. Relatively speaking, everything else was okay in my home. So in December 1995, I went to a doctor in Enugu to seek medical intervention. When that didn't work, I travelled to London the following year, twice even, hoping advanced medicine would help, but nothing did.

When medicine failed, my husband and I turned to God, praying and believing that He would intervene. Yes, I prayed to the same God I did not honour, the same God I thought I was too blessed to serve. One Sunday morning in 1997, I was in bed when a voice said to me, clearly, "Get up and go worship at the Rock Family Church." It was surprising, as I had never attended the church before. But since I knew where it was located, I showered, got dressed and rushed to the church. During the service, while the senior pastor preached, I kept receiving a prompt to step out if an altar call was made. As he preached, I was convicted, so I stepped out immediately he made the altar call.

Two years after that encounter, in 1999, I gave birth to my son. The events surrounding his birth were nothing short of a miracle. The medical team that attended to me was doubtful about his chances. They did not know if he would be a normal baby and live a healthy life. My son was born clinically dead. I was under anaesthesia and did not witness what happened in the delivery room, but from what the medical team told me, they tried to resuscitate him and had almost given up when a breath of life came into him from nowhere. That was not all. After his birth, a nurse hinted to me that because of the cessation of blood and oxygen to his brain before resuscitation, my son might not develop normally. After the miracle, I had heard about his birth, I knew God wasn't done, so I didn't give the nurse a chance to conclude her statement. I responded that she did not know the agreement God and I had made concerning my son. The last thing I needed was to entertain fear, so I trusted God to do another miracle, and He did not disappoint me.

In many ways, my son is a miracle child. Too many incidences reinforced this early enough. One of such was how confident I was about his gender even before any scan revealed it. Long before I had a scan, my husband and I named our baby Chukwuemeka Ifeanyichukwu Daniel. Also, I shopped all-male clothing, insisting that a boy was coming, even when the possibility of carrying a girl was very high. You see, like Hannah in the Bible, I had pleaded with God for a son on the altar of Rock Family Church, Enugu, on December 31, 1997, and I trusted Him to honour my request. He did! Six months after my son's birth, I was called up to resume at the Nigerian Law School in Abuja. I was very excited about it. But when I told my husband about it, he insisted that I defer the admission till the following year. He could not imagine how I would care for a toddler and a 5-year-old child all by myself in Abuja while attending lectures. I also did not know, but I was certain that speaking to God would give me answers. So, I sat by my bed and pleaded with God to teach me how to persuade my husband.

I spoke to God like my biological father, telling Him how much I wanted to go to Law School that year. He had given me the grace to write my first semester exams barely a week after giving birth to my son through Caesarean section. He had also helped me to graduate without any hitch. I knew that if He had done these for me, it was because He had plans for me in the field of law, so I asked Him to soften my husband's heart towards my admission into Law School. God did it! My husband changed his mind and made provisions for the children, their nanny, my personal driver and I to relocate to Abuja. One of my husband's cousins, made her home in Kubwa available to us.

In December 1999, we returned home for Christmas. When it was time to return to Abuja, the nanny refused to return with us. At this time, I had already learnt that any problem could be fixed at God's feet, so I went to God again. Till date, my bedside is where I go to have a father-daughter conversation with God. Apart from the answered prayers, another thing I cherish about my relationship with God is the time I spend alone with Him, like during my long drives to Kubwa from Law School. At times, on that lonely stretch of road, I would feel God's presence in the car.

It would feel like He was seated next to me as I drove, and I knew I was not alone. Once, I started talking to God, telling Him I was tired of driving long distances daily, especially late at night after lectures. God came to my rescue and directed me to a staff of Law School who gave me an alternative, shorter route to and from school. It was a relief because it came at the peak of a fierce battle that raged in my home.

A vehicle knocked down my daughter as she was returning from school. She spent weeks recuperating. On many occasions, I nursed her through the night. Then, I would drive to school the next day half-awake. I cannot deny God's help on those days because if He had not been there for me, I would have lost my life. When I thought the battle was over, after my daughter's recovery, my son took ill. We visited hospital after hospital for answers. He was finally diagnosed with asthma. When I heard it, I did not know what else to feel anything towards God except anger. Why would He do that to me? Many nights, I sat by my son, as he stayed awake in respiratory distress, while still angry at God for allowing it to happen. Overwhelmed by the weight of my anger with the situation, I would sit on the floor of my bedroom and ask God to forgive me for getting angry with Him. And as always, I asked for His help because I had no clue how to handle the situation.

When my husband visited the children and me, he saw first-hand what I was dealing with when it came to our son's health. I remember on one of those nights, we had to drive to Garki Specialist Hospital and National Hospital at about 2 a.m. My husband, inexperienced at such emergencies, couldn't help but panic. He kept asking me, "Is he still breathing?" While this situation continued, people advised us to remove the rugs in our house. They also advised us to stop frying anything. We got a long list of things to avoid. One evening, I returned home from school, exhausted and hungry, only to learn my son had a fever. With no time to waste, I took him to a consultant paediatrician who lived in the same estate with us, thinking we would get another list of medication from him. But the doctor only repeated the same list of things to avoid. That was the height of it! I could not take it anymore. I cried on our way home. My cousin-in-law who drove us said nothing. There are moments when we need to allow people to deal with issues without making ourselves advisors and counsellors. Our silence might be all they need. I made a decision. As we walked in, I left my son in his favourite side of the sitting room. He often sat there to watch other children as they played around the house. I kept him there, and in tears, I told God I was done.

"God," I remember saying, "Thank You for this son You gave me, but I cannot deal with this. I am giving him back to You. He won't sleep in my bed tonight. I will leave him here. It's either You take his life or heal him. When I asked You for a son, did I ask for a son with severe respiratory issues? If I wake up and he's dead, I won't be angry. I will bury him. And if he's alive, please let him be alive and well."

I went to bed feeling utterly exhausted and shattered. I cried myself to sleep. I don't even remember when or how I dozed off, but I slept so peacefully, my first in many months since the ordeal started. Then, I woke up and it was 5 a.m. I ran to the sitting room where I had left my baby and he wasn't there. I panicked! I tiptoed to my cousin-in-law's room and right in her bed was my son, sleeping peacefully by her side. I ran back to my bedroom and went flat on the floor. I didn't say a word as tears poured down my face.

Could it be that he had died? I wondered. Was it possible for him to sleep calmly like that? What was going on? Still on the floor, I dozed off again. The next time I woke up, it was because the noise from the children had disturbed my sleep. When I went to see what they were up to, I saw my son smiling and playing like a perfectly healthy child. I don't know how, but God did it! He made a way! I am writing this only because He made a way.

A few months after the ordeal with my son, my husband took the kids with him to Enugu so I could write my exams. After they arrived, I called them frequently to remind everyone not to use anything with menthol on my son. My worry was pointless because till date, there has been no emergency with him. To d a y , my 21-year-old son is rounding off his first degree in Mechanical Engineering. His life perfectly reflects his names, Chukwuemeka, meaning 'God has done well', and Ifeanyichukwu, meaning 'there is nothing God cannot do'.

It was my desire to have a son and my decision to win the battle over his life that drew me closer to God. I had moments where I strayed from God, yet He kept and shielded me. I have been refined through my experiences. More importantly, I now relate to God as my Father. Nothing should make you doubt God's love for you. He loves us with an everlasting love.

ABOUT THE AUTHOR

US Congress Recognition Award Winner, Gozie C. Udemezue is an Attorney, a human rights activist and holds a Master of Laws Degree in Human Rights Law from Queen Mary College of the University of London. She is an alumna of the US Department of State International Visitors Leadership Program (IVLP) and a fellow of the Africa Leadership Institute of West Africa (ALIWA) under the Aspen global leadership program. She is a renowned global public speaker, covering human rights issues and life. Gozie resides in Enugu, Nigeria with her three amazing children.

12

UNDERNEATH ARE THE EVERLASTING ARMS

BINTA MAX-GBINIJIE

Saturday 22nd June, 2019

As I gazed with contentment out of the small oval window of my seat on the Air Peace domestic flight from Lagos to Abuja that Saturday morning, I was happy to be going home to see my family after having worked the entire week in Lagos. The white clouds wove like tendrils and formed all kinds of interesting shapes to my active imagination. Was it the end span of the wings of an Angel I could see peeking over the wings and fuselage of the metal bird we were flying in? Was that a wavy galloping horse I saw just there? Surely they were!

And I marvelled afresh at the awesomeness of God. As we landed and taxied to a stop at the Abuja airport, I closed my eyes again to thank God for His unfailing protection time and again these last seven years in particular as I had shuttled to and fro from Abuja to Lagos and the many locations all over Nigeria and abroad without an accident or a mishap of any kind. Despite the endless executive hours 'wasted' waiting for delayed flights at all kinds of airports over the years, and the sometimes 'ungodly' hours at which I landed at destinations, I was mindful enough to remain thankful that God had been truly good and kept me these many years on my numerous journeys.

Every time I returned home, it was to find my dwelling in peace with nothing amiss as the Bible had promised and I did not take this privilege for granted at all. I sang praises as I retrieved my luggage from the designated carousel and headed home joyfully to sleep in my own bed that night, see my family and get a much needed rest.

Monday 24th June 2019

Jesus!!! Wayo!!! Mercy!!! God ooooh!!! All kinds of cries and shouts rend the air as the plane was thrown from side to side and whipped about like a paper cup in the turbulence when we ostensibly headed for the Enugu airport. It seemed this flight would not make it there in one piece after all. The lightning flashed, the thunderstorms crashed continuously and the rain came down in heavy sheets and in torrents while every man and woman called on their God and their gods in their various dialects and languages. The plane jumped high, low, swished from side to side and at a point seemed to fall from the sky while the pilot struggled to steady it and take it to its destination.

As I muttered in tongues and prayed out loud, my mind flashed back to just forty-eight hours earlier when that flight had been smooth and the sky like a clear glass. That time when I had gazed complacently outside of the window and reflected on God's awesomeness! Was this then the end? Na here I go die, my Jesus? I cried out, remembering my husband and my children who were still in their respective beds back in Abuja when I left very early that morning to catch that first flight.

Did I even say good-bye properly, my mind questioned? Would they be fine if I don't return home? Oh my God! How will my parents take the loss? Ha! My church family – not again! How could they lose their pastor again in another air crash? But God, You promised me affliction wouldn't arise a second time! How can Trem Vision House mourn again after the Dana air crash took their former pastors whom we replaced in Abuja? God, no! Nooooo Jesus! I had done this shuttle for almost seven years. I've been in the air, on the road and on the train tracks too, more recently for practically every single week of those seven years and God had preserved me all these many days through sun, rain, and high waters.

Had that perhaps made me believe I will never go this way, holding strongly unto my faith that as I had hitherto constantly decreed, I will live to be a hundred years in good health, plenty of wealth and great joy with my children's children like Olive plants around my table as the Bible had promised?

This was not the plan Lord! I fearfully reminded God. Remember my plans, which I jocularly shared with anyone who cared to listen Father? You remember, nau Lord, that after my 100th birthday celebration where I would be the funkiest glammest great-grandma ever? I would, like Jacob in Genesis 49:33, "finish commanding... draw my feet up into the bed and be gathered unto my people?"

Remember my thoughtful plan to go on that day after the celebrations while my children and grandchildren from all continents would still be around. How I would save them all money, time and energy, as they would not need to go back to Canada, the USA and wherever they would have come from for my birthday only to return again for my funeral. But I will ensure I pass peacefully while they are still around in Nigeria to kill two birds with one stone for their sakes and how in fact, they can use the same outfits for the funeral and save *Aso-ebi* money there too as the prudent banker in me would prefer? God! This was not the plan oooh, not to end up in an unmarked watery grave somewhere or my body shattered into smithereens over the skies in the east or lost forever in some forest the plane might crash-land into with no cadaver to deliver to my family. There would be no closure if they don't have a whole body to bury. Surely God, not now, not like this? I tearfully reasoned with my Creator.

These thoughts all swirled around in my head within split seconds but with scary ferocity as the plane continued to career and hurtle downwards seemingly about to disintegrate or crash-land. I almost peed in my black trousers as the elements tugged at the plane and the battle between nature and the captain raged unabated for what seemed like an eternity. I pondered if this was indeed the end.

Was this what one of my favourite heroines in the Bible felt at that scary time in her life as well, I wondered? Did her life flash before her eyes as she scurried to avert the impending death of her household at the hand of the avenging King David because of Nabal and his unimaginable refusal to accede to the reasonable request from the King? 2Samuel25:2-13.

Abigail hurried into action and did not allow the looming disaster befall her family. As the wise woman she was, she took presents to appease the sin and ran ahead to meet Kind David with his soldiers who were headed to her city and her home for what would undoubtedly have been a bloodbath, unimaginable carnage with the attendant loss of lives. She intercepted him before the disaster was unleashed and said to him in verses 31, 32 and 35:

> ³¹*I pray thee, forgive the trespass of thine handmaid: for the LORD will certainly make my lord a sure house; because my lord fighteth the battles of the LORD, and evil hath not been found in thee all thy days.*
> ³²*And David said to Abigail, Blessed be the LORD God of Israel, which sent thee this day to meet me:*
> ³⁵*So David received of her hand that which she had brought him, and said unto her, Go up in peace to thine house; see, I have hearkened to thy voice, and have accepted thy person."*

That might have been the end of her family had Abigail not hasted to do the right thing to the saving of her household, preventing collateral damage and who knows, perhaps the end of her own life too.

What about queen Esther? What was her state of mind when she heard of the evil Haman's plans for her people and her race? She must have died many deaths before she decided to take her destiny in hand and ended up making that profound famous statement: "If I perish, I perish".

They did not perish, thankfully, so Father, neither will I today. I determined with new faith sparking to life in my heart as I remembered my covenant of life and reminded God of it with growing confidence. Not today Lord, not today. *I will NOT DIE but live to declare the wondrous works of the Most High in the Land of the living.* You have saved me these many years on countless journeys and even today. Underneath this plane are Your everlasting arms so we will touch down safely. We MUST! I decreed it with growing boldness but just then, the plane nose-dived abruptly, in the enemy's bid to jolt and scare me out of my loud confessions. Because the devil is a liar and only God has the power, I raised my voice decibels higher and like blind Bartimeaus at the gate of

Jericho, I shouted much louder – JESUS! Thou Son of David, have mercy on me!

After an almost endless interlude, God in His mercy, heard the cries of the multitude in the plane and allowed us break free of that turbulence into a more manageable weather. The pilot eventually won this round and nature had no choice but to concede and acquiesce, releasing the aircraft to eventually land at the Akanu Ibiam International Airport in the heavy rain with on-going raucous and un-abating prayers, cries, chants and all manner of soliloquies of the diverse passengers on board. We all disembarked on rubbery feet with tears streaming down the faces of some people who had literally been to hell and back in the less than sixty minutes tumultuous experience in the air. Some could not speak, some had to be physically assisted and helped off the plane and others could only manage to mutter THANK YOU JESUS! CHUKWU DAALU! JESU, E MA SE! UBANGIJI MUN GODE! ABASI OSONG!! Out of shaky lips. I had heard all kinds of colourful expletives, different languages and dialects that day which made the whole experience even more surreal as we struggled to process what had almost just happened.

My introspection continued and I thought long and hard as I was driven away from the airport that day thankful that indeed underneath were His everlasting arms. But, what if this had truly been the last day of my life? Was I ready and were my affairs in order with an updated Will? Was my family in the know on how to deal with my demise? Had I imparted enough into my sons to make them heaven-bound or left them a legacy to be proud of yet? Did they know my intentions about how I would like to be buried or how my "techere" assets were to be distributed and who my preferred beneficiaries should be? Will my office do the needful regarding my entitlements and make it very easy for my family particularly since I was on official duty for the bank on this trip? Had I settled all issues and resolved all grievances, if any? Just the day before, I had confronted a sister in church who had just betrayed me in what I considered a spectacular fashion and as you know, sometimes it is those closest to us that can hurt us the most.   Betrayal and disappointment sting and I had, in my vexed state, told her in no uncertain terms to stay away from my family and me.

In the light of eternity, was that truly the right step to take in cutting her off as it were? Had I made amends where I had offended anyone myself and asked for their forgiveness or apologised in true contrition? The Bible urges us to leave our sacrifice at the altar and go make amends before we come back and pray. Had all my sacrifices before that day been acceptable to God or were some of them *Ichabod*? Had I made good all my pledges and my vows unto the Lord or were there some as yet unredeemed? Did I owe anyone anything other than love? Had I told everyone I loved that I did love or admire them, or told some who needed home truths what they needed to know or had I enabled their dependencies and not helped them by keeping quiet?

Had my soul-winning efforts been commendable and on course? Had I been wise enough since the Bible confirms that *he that winneth a soul is wise*? Had I been 'foolish' by not preaching the gospel enough in season and out of season as advocated? Did I live the talk and walk the walk enough as a true ambassador of the most High God and draw men to my King or had I perhaps, even inadvertently, 'driven' some away from the faith by any thoughtless word or by my actions? Mercy Lord! I cried out.

Peradventure I was guilty of some of these actions by commission or by omission. Mercy Lord! In true anguish of soul, I pleaded for forgiveness from the Lord regarding where I might have missed it.

I asked that He purge away all the sins I may have committed or where I might have failed to do the right thing. I pleaded that the precious soul cleansing Blood of the Lamb wash away every iniquity and transgression far away from me.

I prayed in self-flagellation until I finally received the calming assurance that my fervent petitions had been heard and my prayers attended to by my Father in Heaven.

Friend, can you answer these questions in the positive and affirmative ways and do you today have a conscience that is void of offence towards God and man? Should the trumpet sound for you today, will you be ready to face your Maker?

That fateful plane ride of Monday 24th June, reminded me of so many things I needed to do and to do quickly, and so much more I also had to jettison to enter fully into what God had in store for me. It was a brutal wake-up call that I badly needed (even though the message could definitely have been delivered in a lot less scary way, that's for sure. Lol. It spurred me on to take some life-enhancing decisions and to ensure balance in my life going forward. I was reminded that my utmost desire and over-arching aim at the end of my time here on earth was to die empty having fulfilled my God-given purpose and completed my earthly assignment.

To easily find my name written in the Lamb's book of life when I stand at the pearly gates, to make Heaven taking as many with me as is possible and most importantly to hear God say to me "well done, thou good and faithful servant, Binta Oluwabunmi Immanuela, enter into the rest and joy of thy Lord".

May this be your beautiful reality also whenever your time on earth is up and may we walk those beautiful streets of gold together in the by and by after we have overcome in Jesus name!

ABOUT THE AUTHOR

Binta Max-Gbinjie is an experienced Financial services Executive with knowledge of the financial services value chain. She holds close to thirty years of experience in strategic leadership, wholesale and retail banking, wealth and fiduciary management, treasury marketing and asset management. She is a pioneer Chief Executive for Stanbic IBTC Trustees Limited. She is a frequent conference speaker on the topics of Faith, the girl child, women's issues, financial literacy and Inclusion.

She is currently an Executive Council Member of Women in Business; Management & Public Service (WIMBIZ). She was the Chairperson Stanbic IBTC Blue Women, Vice President of The Association of Corporate Trustees and was voted in 2018 as one of Nigeria's Most Inspiring Women. She is married with children.

13

TRASH TO TREASURE

DAMOLA TREASURE OKENLA

"And then, after your brief suffering, the God of all loving grace, who has called you to share in His eternal glory in Christ, will personally and powerfully restore you and make you stronger than ever. Yes, He will set you firmly in place and build you up." (1 Peter 5:10)

I received the scripture above in a revelation one morning in 2000, and it was confirmed the same day by a friend who, though was a new believer, was always praying for me. I thought it was a word for overcoming whatever struggle I might be in at the time, not knowing the suffering was waiting for me in another country entirely. Later on, somebody said to me while laughing, "Oyinda, you don't understand English. If you do, you would have known that the pain was yet to take place at the time you had the revelation." Indeed, the interpretation was clear. It was an ordeal for the future.

I have been a devoted prayer intercessor and an associate pastor in church, and have heard the Spirit of Lord instruct me to help certain people. Even though I wasn't exactly definite about whom these persons were, the instructions came clearly, being confirmed by a line of scripture in Isaiah 42:6-7. But then, I was going to understand better as events later unpacked.

My birth name is Oyindamola Adetura, but I was on a journey where I would be rechristened "Treasure" as was later revealed by God. I was thirty-seven when I was introduced to a serial married man, unknown to me at the time, though. I was told he never married and had no children – what every good, single lady wanted. Also, I was made to believe he had strived to marry different women who only dated him for their material needs and later abandoned him. He was told I would help him because I'm not just a Christian, but also a pastor. There was no way I would mess him up.

"Yes, this is my chance, and I must catch it at once," I said to myself. I was already having it hard with family pressure, and the constant rants of "a woman's biological clock does not wait". I fell under the pressure, deciding to stick with a man who was not meant for me. During the four months of our phone conversations, I never asked any real questions, having fallen for misgivings about his supposed devoted and fervent Christian life.

I was going through a phase in my relationship with God. I felt He had disappointed me, and I wanted revenge. So I did not pray about the relationship, thinking there was no point, since all God had promised me previously did not come to pass. But it is the same God I turned to eventually when things did not work out as expected. And praise unto Him, He did not ridicule me, but instead, He accepted me and helped me out.

My new suitor never seemed threatened by the fulfilment of God's call upon my life, of which I was afraid many men, even pastors, would ask me to stop after marriage. I had my selfish reasons. He talked about how he would support me and talked about prayer.

Alas, my newfound love interest came to Nigeria and we went to the registry. And after that, I got a shocker that the marriage certificate could not be used for any formal documentation because my supposed husband still had a marriage in existence. So, he divorced the other woman. I didn't understand the implication until later. I thought as a Christian, I was to stay. He promised we would have the legal solemnization of the marriage when I relocated to the US. Things happened very fast, and I moved to the US with him, leaving all I had behind including my business, for I was one of the foremost event planners in Nigeria at the time. The City People Magazine always featured my work with the headline, "From Oyin Okenla's Matchmates Concepts".

Things changed so rapidly. There was no room for me to overcome my travel fatigue before the hardest reality hit me. It was nothing I expected could ever happen to me. I became stranded with no immediate support from the one who had invited me. He was looking for a cash cow, and he had found that in me. Much to my disappointment, marriage never improved with him. Our seven years together were moments torn apart, more like coping with a great inferno in the living room. I can only now describe those years as times of slavery, of emotional, financial, and social abuse. We lived as strangers, roommates, bill sharers - with me as the cook, errand girl, cleaner and no support from him.

Questions that raced through my mind included, "God, why did you allow me to come here ? Why didn't you stop me? After all, You have stopped me before."

I was angry with myself. I felt lonely and abandoned. My husband was an unfriendly friend, a total stranger who was not interested in my welfare but in what he could get from me. I don't think we ever sat down to converse like a man to a woman except if he had to send me on errands. There was no relationship at all. Sometimes, I would just scream in the house. I felt low. I lost my dignity for a moment. Unknown to me, some people in my church were laughing at me behind my back, and some pitied me, wondering how I got involved with such a man. Of course, that weighed me down. However, I believed I walked into the marriage and had to live with it. I knew things were not right, but I thought, as a Christian, it was my cross to bear. I accepted it as my fate. Another shocker was that he was not a Christian at all. He just used Christianese to deceive me. A different lie he told me was he was a Molecular Biologist. I later found out he only had an associate degree from a junior college.

The man talked derogatorily about me to anybody who cared to listen. When they advised him to let me go, he would reply, "She is a Christian, and Christians don't leave. I have tried everything to frustrate her but she refuses to go." He was right. All I could think about was how things could get better.

Two years into the union, I discovered he was sending a lot of money to a lady in Nigeria, not the one he eventually married. When I confronted him, he apologised, and that was the only time he ever gave me a gift. Anyway, outsiders could see the problem I was in and advised me to leave. Again, I would respond by saying, "I'm a Christian". All I could think and pray about was a dramatic transformation. I didn't realise the guy was formed in his ways and was not ready to bend.

He tried to discourage me from going to church, but he failed because I was grounded in my relationship with Christ; there was no room for settling. I remained ever committed to my service in the church as the prayer ministry coordinator. My service became my solace. I surely didn't allow my predicament to get to the surface or dampen my spiritual life. I eventually got a decent job; it was with an insurance company that had a very comprehensive insurance package covering an IVF procedure. My pastor advised that I should go for it. My husband followed me to the fertility centre, but he refused to follow up with the process, and they could not continue the process without his consent since I already presented him as my spouse. I realised later on that he had zero sperm count.

A month before God would finally set me free from that entanglement, I was at a friend's place in Atlanta where I was participating in a 21-day prayer and fasting exercise. On the twentieth day, God said to me, "I have called you TREASURE." In my bewilderment, I knew God was calling me for something bigger outside of that marriage, but I was too concerned about what the world would say if I decided to leave. I didn't want my silent sufferings to come to the notice and scornful attention of the public.

Meanwhile, I had had a series of dreams and revelations that God wasn't going to bless that union and that I needed to move on. But I jettisoned all of that until the biggest shocker came.

On the January 9th, 2011, the door opened for me to go. He was away in Nigeria for Christmas. He had gone to marry another lady. While he was away, God instructed me to go on eight days of praise, which I did. My husband returned on the ninth day, and I was bold to confront him. I wanted to know what would happen to me since he had married someone else. He responded that I should go back to Nigeria. At that instant, I felt like killing somebody. I picked up my things and headed to an older church member's' house. And that was the end of that phase and the beginning of a completely new journey.

I wanted to settle in a law court, but God said, "No. You have the power to destroy, but you cannot." So I rested my case, allowing God to take His course. Little did I know that that was my moment of epiphany and divine turn-around. That bitter experience became my way of escape from seven years of slavery and suffering and also became the start of a new era in my calling and purpose.

At the end of the storm came my calm. The result was evident in the founding of Divine Connections Seminars and Workshops, a program I set up to save marriages before they start and to help singles not enter into wrong relationships.

If God is the one leading you, He will sustain you. He is the All-sufficient One. For almost three years, while I was trying to find my bearing, I had free accommodation. I was able to pay off my car despite having no steady income. God stationed many angels along the way. That was why I titled my fiftieth birthday autobiography, *Many Acts of Kindness*. It's been nine years now, and I can testify to the goodness of God.

I have been able to help many young ladies through my seminars and workshops and through several of my books to avoid the same mistakes that I've made. There are also testimonies from couples who have enjoyed tremendous peace in their marriages, courtesy of God's work through my organisation.

The testimony is that 'God turned trash to treasure', which is now evident in my new name. Throughout the season, I was conscious of my purpose and how not to miss it. I'm still on the journey of destiny; my life and time are in His hands. God works behind the scenes of our lives, and sometimes, we may not understand the journey, but trusting Him to lead the way makes our path smooth and successful. Who would have known it was God who had orchestrated that supposedly rough road which Joseph had walked en-route fame in a strange land?

THE SCRIPTURAL SOLACE

"For our light and momentary afflictions are attaining for us an eternal glory that far outweighs them all." (2 Corinthians 4 verse 17).

The scriptures have given every answer we need to pass every phase of our lives. All that is required of us is to find these answers and find solace in them. It doesn't usually stop at finding these portions of God's words. Many have seen it, but it didn't benefit them. As the book of Hebrews 4:2 says: "For surely we have had the good news [of salvation] preached unto us, just as the Israelites also [when the good news of the promised land came to them]; but the message they heard did not profit them, because it did not mix with faith [in God] by those who heard," cliffing unto God's divine promises for us works the magic. In circumstances where we feel alone, betrayed, and wounded inside and outside, there are innumerable scriptural instructions on how to deal with such situations.

First, be sure that times of afflictions don't last. "For our light and momentary troubles are achieving for us an eternal glory that far outweighs them all." (2 Corinthians 4:17) What this means is that darkness cannot comprehend the light. You're a light, and so difficult times can't survive you. Two, always remember that God's plan for you is to come out of every situation as a winner. "For I know the thoughts I have for you," declares the Lord, "thoughts to prosper you and not to harm you, plans to give you hope and a future." (Jeremiah 29:11). Every situation you are passing through works for your good, if only you believe. The word of God corroborates this. Also, when God vindicates you, be careful not to repay evil with evil. Vengeance is God's. Joseph gave room for divine justice. He didn't fight for himself; the same way we too cannot fight for ourselves. Leaving God to take charge for us is the surest way to cruise to victory. One with God is a majority.

I don't know what God has birthed into your spirit that has taken an extended time to see the light of the day. All I know is those things will come to pass if only you will trust Him. Men may have disappointed you along the way, but trust God to send the needful help to you along the journey. Trust his leading (Psalm 32:8).

Your problem cannot cancel your purpose. I've discovered our problems are sometimes the pointers to our missions. If I stayed in Nigeria, I would probably have concentrated on accumulating wealth. There was no way I would have thought of helping singles, absolutely no way. But remember how my peace was kept in much turbulence and afflictions. Trust God with your purpose and He will make it count for you. His frame inevitably brings fame from shame.

Your pain, your mistake, your failures don't define you and cannot confine you. However, like Joseph, you push towards the fulfilment of your dream.
God is not a waster of resources. Your past mistakes and experiences are all raw materials in the hand of God to make you become who He has ordained you to be.

Trust God with your missteps, and He can bring miracles out of them in your life as well as the lives of those around you.

No matter your situation, you must be conscious of your purpose, and it must form your primary focus and goal. Be sensitive to it. Don't downplay your connections. They are the bridges God wants to use for your advantage. Maintaining a good relationship with everyone who crosses your path is pivotal to the fulfilment of destinies. On the night I left my apartment for Atlanta, the efficacy of this statement played out. God used my friends and a couple of people as instruments for His glory.

So, do not jettison human relationships. Finally, I am confident that although I may not be married yet, I'm fulfilling God's purpose for my life because I have learned to entrust all to His care, knowing He will use my life for His glory. All of my experiences have taught me to trust God for the best in whatever situation I am going through. Whether they are the darkest of times or very hollow moments, one thing is sure: God doesn't fail anyone.

ABOUT THE AUTHOR
Damola Treasure Okenla As an award-winning author of several Christian books and a highly sought-after inspirational speaker, Damola Treasure Okenla is dedicated to uplifting others mentally, spiritually, and emotionally. As the president and founder of Life Encounters, Inc., a non-profit organization that is dedicated to self-discovery and recovery, Damola facilitates seminars, workshops and retreats to usher others into purpose fulfillment. She serves as the president and founder of Hilltop Publishing, where she assists Christian authors with publishing and social media management for their book projects—positioning them for excellence in the marketplace. Damola works as an accountant and project manager and holds a Master's in Public Administration. More than anything, Damola is on a mission.

14

AFTERWORD

The only reason we can go through many troubles and still stand is because we trust God. You have read our ridiculously fantastic, sometimes challenging stories and you must have noticed the theme of *trust* running through. The victory at the end is what we celebrate. Trust in God gave us staying power through it all.

The life of a Christian is not easy, yet it is fun, exciting, challenging, fulfilling and rewarding. Sometimes it gets worse, sometimes it is incredibly wonderful but most times it's just great. Life is what it is, but when you've got God on your side, you're not only winning battles here, you're prepared for eternity with Him.

We invite you to, please, accept Jesus today by saying this prayer:

Lord Jesus, I realise that I'm a sinner. I come to You today to ask that You forgive me of all my sins and cleanse me of all unrighteousness. Come into my heart today and be my Lord and Saviour in Jesus' name.

If you said this prayer and mean it from you heart, voila! You're now a born-again child of God. You need to find and join a Bible-believing church in your area. You need to grow by being fed with the Word of God.
Congratulations!

15

CALL FOR SUBMISSION

We hope you were blessed reading this book. Did it speak to your heart? Did it encourage you? Did it inspire you? Were you motivated? We would love to hear from you. This is book three of THE TRUST CHRONICLES. Have you read the first two books in the series? Anchored By Trust and The Hand You Hold are available on Amazon and other local bookstores.

Would you love to share your *trust* story and contribute to the next trust book in the series? Kindly send an email to thetrustchronicles@gmail.com and we will contact you with our submission guidelines. We cannot wait to read your trust story. You can also visit our social media pages:

Facebook: http//facebook.com/thetrustchronicles/
Instagram: https://instagram.com/thetrustchronicles
Twitter: https://twitter.com/trustchronicles
YouTube: @thetrustchronicles

Beautiful in His time

Printed in Great Britain
by Amazon